D1098970

Stellar Quines Theatre Company presents

The Unconquered
by Torben Betts

First performance at the Byre Theatre of St Andrews, Scotland, on 14 February 2007
Initial tour to 21 venues in Scotland and England from 14 February – 31 March 2007

A production in association with the Byre Theatre of St Andrews

Supported and sponsored by:

Redding Park
Development Co. Ltd.

Scottish
Arts Council

Scottish Executive
New Arts Sponsorship Awards
in conjunction with
A&B
Arts & Business Scotland

Highlands & Islands
ENTERPRISE

THE BYRE THEATRE
of St. Andrews

Cast

Girl Pauline Turner
Mother Jane Guernier
Father Kevin McMonagle
Soldier Nigel Barrett

Creative Team

Playwright Torben Betts
Director Muriel Romanes
Co-Director/Movement A C Wilson
Visual Artist and Designer Keith McIntyre
Lighting Designer Jeanine Davies
Sound Designer Pete Vilk
Voice Coach Linda Wise
Costume Maker and Associate Visual Artist Cat Maddocks

Production, Management & Crew

Production Manager Stephen Sinclair (Byre Theatre)
Master Carpenter Ron Kiddel
Freelance Wardrobe Supervisor Kirsteen Naismith
General Manager Alexandra Stampler-Brown (Stellar Quines)
Administrator Kirsty Vidler (Stellar Quines)
Press & PR London Dan Pursey (Mobius)

Company Stage Manager Danni Bastian
Deputy Stage Manager Emma Skaer
Technical Stage Manager Claire Bromhead

Cast Biographies

Pauline Turner *Girl*

Pauline trained at the Webber Douglas Academy. Theatre includes *Miss Julie/Measure For Measure* (Peter Hall Company), *Men Should Weep* (Oxford Stage Company), *Bread and Butter* (OSC and Tricycle Theatre), *Sun is Shining* (BAC and Brits off Broadway Festival, NY), *Top Girls* (Citizens Theatre, Glasgow), *Mill on the Floss* (Shared Experience/tour and West End), *The Importance of Being Earnest* (Theatre Clwyd, Birmingham Rep and Princess of Wales Theatre, Toronto), *The Prime of Miss Jean Brodie* (Theatre of Comedy/tour and West End), *The Champion of Paribanou* (Stephen Joseph Theatre Scarborough), *Emma* and *Borders of Paradise* (Watford Palace Theatre), *Incarcerator* and *Three Girls in Blue* (White Bear Theatre), *You Never Can Tell*, *Joking Apart*, *A Flea in Her Ear*, *The Rehearsal* and *Vie de Boheme* (Pitlochry Festival Theatre) *Lavender Blue* and *Phaedra* (Royal Lyceum Theatre Edinburgh). Television and film include *Young Adam* (Hanway/Warner Brothers), *Goodnight Mister Tom* (Carlton), *Taggart* (STV), *Whycliff* and *Heartbeat* (ITV), *Martin Chuzzlewit*, *Two Thousand Acres of Sky*, *Casualty*, *Bad Boys* and *The Key* (BBC).

Jane Guernier *Mother*

Theatre includes: *Interior* and *Winners* (The Young Vic), *Brand* (Royal Shakespeare Company) and *Love and Other Fairy Tales*, *Paper Walls, Sisters and Others, New Lives* and *Stranded* (Scarlet Theatre Company). Jane originally trained in physical theatre and has often worked with John Wright and Told By An Idiot on comic shows such as *A Little Fantasy, An Evening with Johnny Springer* and *The Last Present*. *Bag Lady* directed by Roxana Silbert, Comic Turns (Paines Plough), and various mask shows with Trestle. Television and film include: Susan Decker in *Dalziel and Pascoe*; Mrs Lawrence in *Murder Prevention*; Joanna in *Hello You* for Fecund Films; *Passer By* and *Hustle*.

Kevin McMonagle *Father*

Kevin McMonagle grew up in Glasgow, was inspired to work in theatre by small-scale touring companies visiting the city during the seventies and consequently trained for the stage in the early eighties at Drama Centre London. His stage work has included seasons at Coventry, Edinburgh, Glasgow, Leeds, Leicester, Liverpool, Manchester, Paris, Stratford. In London he has worked at the Soho, the Bush, the Gate, Battersea, the Royal Court and the National Theatre. He has wide experience both as a Guest and Principal in many radio and television dramas including *Bramwell* (Whitby/Davison), *Krakatoa The Last Days* (BBC Science), Inspector Morse (Zenith), *Quite Ugly One Morning* (Clerkenwell), *Your Cheatin Heart* (BBC), *The Pallisers, The Immortals, The Bayeux Tapestry* (BBC R4). Now this is his first full small/mid-scale tour.

Nigel Barrett *Soldier*

Nigel Barrett trained at Drama Studio. Recent work includes *Mud Man* and *Beverly + Mae* (Shunt), *The High Road* (National Theatre Studio), *Mirror For Princes* (Barbican), *Bold man in a Boat* (TV), *Amato Saltone* and *Tropicana* (Shunt/National Theatre) and *The Influence* (Radio 4). Nigel has appeared in two of Torben Betts's previous plays: *Five Visions of the Faithful* (White Bear Theatre, London) and *Incarcerator* (BAC, London).

Artistic Team Biographies

Torben Betts *Playwright*

Plays include: *A Listening Heaven* (SJT, Scarborough & Edinburgh Royal Lyceum); *Incarcerator* (White Bear Theatre & BAC, both London); *Five Visions of the Faithful* (White Bear & Edinburgh Fringe Festival); *Clockwatching* (SJT and Orange Tree Theatre, Richmond); *The Biggleswades* (White Bear & Southwark Playhouse); *Silence and Violence* (White Bear); *The Last Days of Desire* (BBC Radio 4); *Spurning Comfort* (Oldham Coliseum Studio); *The Trough* (Kuwait International Theatre Festival 2002); *Her Slightest Touch* (SJT); *The Lunatic Queen* (Riverside Studios); *The Optimist; The Error of Their Ways; This is Glorious; The Misfortune of Martha Mcleod; Mummies and Daddies* and *The Company Man*. He was the writer-in-residence at the SJT in 1999 and *The Swing of Things* opens there this summer, while a major tour of *A Listening Heaven* is currently being planned for the autumn of 2007. Three volumes of his plays are published by Oberon Books, London.

Muriel Romanes *Director*

Muriel Romanes has had over thirty years' experience in theatre both as an actress and director and was Associate Director at the Royal Lyceum Theatre in Edinburgh, where she has directed several acclaimed productions, including *The Deep Blue Sea, A Listening Heaven, Lavender Blue, A Streetcar Named Desire*, the highly successful *The Prime of Miss Jean Brodie* by Muriel Spark, a Scots translation by Martin Bowman and Bill Findlay of Michele Tremblay's *If Only* and most recently *Anna Karenina*. Muriel has been with Stellar Quines since 1993 and since 1996 has been the Artistic Director. She has directed for Stellar Quines, *The Clearing* by Helen Edmundson, *The Reel of the Hanged Man* by Jean-Mance Delisle, *Sweet Fanny Adams in Eden* by Judith Adams, *The Memory of Water* by Shelagh

Stephenson and most recently *Three Thousand Troubled Threads* by Chiew Siah Tei as part of the Edinburgh International Festival 2005.

A C Wilson
Co-Director/Movement

A C Wilson began working as an actor, director and teacher. After graduating from St Andrew's University, he trained at the Royal Welsh College of Music and Drama, and the Ecole Lecoq, Paris. His performance, directing and teaching work has taken him to Finland, Germany, Austria, Greece, Japan and the United States. His direction credits began simultaneously at the Edinburgh Festival Fringe with *How To Kill*, a Fringe First Winner, and in Innsbruck Austria with *A Mouthful of Birds, Salome, The Balcony* and *The Human Voice*. His recent work in London includes Torben Betts' *The Biggleswades* (Southwark Playhouse – where he was also Resident Assistant Director and Literary Associate), and rehearsed readings of new works by Betts including *This is Glorious* and *The Error of Their Ways* (Theatre 503, London) and *The Misfortunes of Martha McLeod* (Net Curtains Theatre Co). He is an associate director of Net Curtains Theatre Co, for whom he directed two new short plays, *Not Waving but Drowning* by Sue Lenier and *1:19* by Tim Stimpson (The Arcola Theatre, London). In September he co-devised and directed the world premiere of the large-scale outdoor show *Perfect Circle* (Emergency Exit Arts). His work in 2007 will include the full-size *1:19* (The Arcola Theatre for Net Curtains Theatre Co), and *The Viewing Room* by Daniel Rubin (Practicum Theatre in London). In Scotland he has directed *Biohazard, Contracts* and *David's Gift* (Theatre Workshop), *Maister Michael* and *The False Alarm* (Borders Festival) and *Killing Times* (Rowan Tree Theatre Company). He recently graduated with Distinction from the Master of Fine Arts in Theatre

Directing from Birkbeck College, University of London.

Keith McIntyre
Visual Artist and Designer

Keith McIntyre studied Fine Art at the Duncan of Jordan Stone College of Arts in Dundee. Drawing is a core element of his practice and increasingly he has been exploring new synergies between graphic fine art media and theatre. He has been visual art director on a number of collaborative projects including *Jock Tamsons Bairns* (Tramway Glasgow, 1990 European City of Culture), *Legend of St Julian* (Traverse, Edinburgh Festival), *Songs for the Falling Angel* (Lockerbie Requiem), *Rites* (Scottish Chamber Orchestra), *Mfalme Juha* (Parapanda Arts Lab. Tanzania + East Africa tour), *New Constellations for Wind, Reed and Drawing Instruments* (BALTIC Centre for Contemporary Art and Sage Gateshead) and *HEID* (Sounds of Progress). Keith McIntyre's paintings, drawings and prints have been exhibited in solo and group exhibitions throughout the world including Glasgow, Edinburgh, London, New York, Copenhagen, Toronto, Havana, Berlin and Milan. His work is represented in many public and private collections including the Scottish National Gallery of Modern Art, SAC, Edinburgh, Glasgow, Dundee and Aberdeen City Collections and Contemporary Arts Trust. He is a previous winner of the Scottish Open Drawing competition. Recently he collaborated with the acclaimed children's writer David Almond and actor Kevin Whately to create *The Savage*, an ITV documentary in partnership with the Seven Stories Centre for Children's Books. Since 1993 he has been living and working in the Newcastle/Gateshead region and is a Reader in Visual Arts at Northumbria University.

Jeanine Davies *Lighting Designer*

Jeanine works regularly at the Royal Lyceum, Edinburgh and most recently on *All My Sons, Les Liaisons Dangereuses, Tartuffe, Laurel and Hardy, Look Back in Anger* (and Bath), *A Madman Sings to the Moon, Uncle Varrick* and *Misery Guts* as well as *Cat on a Hot Tin Roof*, which has also been on UK tour. Other work in Scotland includes *Tutti Frutti* and *Hansel and Gretel* (National Theatre Scotland), *Lifeboat* (UK and USA, Catherine Wheels); *The Bevellers* (Glasgow Citz); *The Talented Mr Ripley, Gypsy, Sweet Bird of Youth* and *Macbeth* (Dundee Rep); *Peter Pan; Lareigne* and *Uncanny* (X Factor Dance Company); *The Woman Who Cooked Her Husband* (tour); *The Memorandum, Zlata's Diary* (Communicado); *Off Kilter* (Dancebase); *Don Pasquale* (Scottish Opera Go Round); *Ay Carmela* (Traverse); *Hamlet* (Brunton); and 2005 Pitlochry season. Other work includes *Tom's Midnight Garden* (opening the new Unicorn Children's Theatre, London and previously UK tour & New York); *The BFG* and *Rat Pack Confidential* (West End); *The Life of Ronnie and Ryan* (tour); *To Reach the Clouds. Polygraph* (Nottingham Playhouse); *Stone City Blues* (Theatre Clwyd); *Clockwork* (ROH Linbury Studio); *A Christmas Carol* (Derby); *Beauty and the Beast* (Cochrane) and *Il Re Pastore* (Classical Opera).

Pete Vilk *Sound Designer*

Pete is a Drummer/Percussionist, Sound Designer, Improviser/Performer and Educator (sometimes all at the same time!). Pete studied with master musicians from West Africa, Brazil, Cuba and Iran and at *DrumTech*, London. Between 1996 and 2000 he established acclaimed community music and performance projects in places as varied as Bosnia & Herzegovina, Republic of Georgia, Turkey and Iran. Recent compositions for theatre music & sound design are *Monster's Tears* and *GoodSisterBad* (Lung Ha's Theatre Company 2005/2006), and *Murder in Birnam* (Refraction/Stepping Stone Theatre Companies) for the opening of Perth Concert Hall 2005. As a specialist tutor, he has worked with Scottish Chamber Orchestra; lectures in 'Group Improvisation' on the Music Therapy Masters at Queen Margaret University College and created the 'Community Music Studies' module at Stevenson College Edinburgh. He plays drum kit and records with Edinburgh-based world music band *GOL*, afro-funk-rock group *Den Collective* and the 14-piece cutting-edge electro-acoustic Brewhouse Band. *GOL – Red Earth* (Artifact Records) is available on iTunes. **www.petevilk.com** Special thanks: Roxana Pope, Sean Williams, Eugene Skeef, Miro.

Catriona Maddocks *Costume Maker and Associate Visual Artist*

Catriona Maddocks graduated from Northumbria University with a BA (Hons) in Fine Art in July 2006. She has been combining her fine art skills with theatre for over three years, most recently working on *Life, Stories, Dreams* with Sounds of Progress and the Scottish National Theatre and *The Firebird*, a production by the Northumberland Theatre Company. Through her art practice she creates ambiguous animalistic sculpture and costumes, exploring relationships between art, theatre, costume and life.

Linda Wise *Voice Coach*

Linda Wise, actress, director and teacher, was born in Kenya and trained at RSAMDA. She is co-director with Enrique Pardo of Pantheatre and the Myth & Theatre Festival, a company based in Paris. She worked with Roy Hart from 1969 until his death in 1975. She was a member of the original Roy Hart Theatre and a founding member of the Roy Hart Centre in the South of France. She is invited to direct and teach throughout the world. She won the 1988 French Vilar prize for her direction of *Moby Dick* and played Nedda in the OBIE award-winning production of Leoncavallo's *Pagliacci*. She has recently directed a Jazz Opera, co-produced with the Oslo National Theatre, *Cabaret Brechtiano* in Chile and a series of solos for women performers. In March 2007 she will direct a devised performance of *Abelard and Heloise* for NYV experimental theatre wing. Passionately concerned with a vision of the voice that engages the widest possible perspective on each person's individuality, she incorporates into her practice a range of vocal approaches, from Roy Hart's extended vocal techniques to bel canto.

Stellar Quines Theatre Company

Stellar Quines Theatre Company facilitates the creative work of women in Scottish Theatre. The company discovers, nurtures, produces and promotes the work of women playwrights, directors, actors, designers and technicians and gives special attention to work which is of relevance to women.

Stellar Quines was formed in 1993 to stimulate, support and enable women to take control of their professional lives. We foster a friendly, collaborative working environment with shared creative vision, resulting in genuinely communal ownership of thought-provoking, brave and high quality theatre.

'A company with amazing depths of energy, maturity and skill.'
Scotland on Sunday

Embracing new art forms in the development of our work, we explore the boundaries between conventional theatre and dance, music, physical theatre and new media.

'Stellar Quines – the dynamic theatre powerhouse synonymous with thinking person's productions.' *Caledonia Magazine*

Stellar Quines has been delighting audiences with entertaining and thought-provoking theatre, touring their most recent successes *The Memory of Water* (2004), *Three Thousand Troubled Threads* (Edinburgh International Festival 2005) and *Perfect Pie* (2006) to critical acclaim.

We encourage new writing through our commissions and facilitate a higher profile for writers. The Unconquered has been developed through our 'Rehearsal Room' initiative at the Traverse Theatre, Edinburgh, with two public readings in spring and autumn 2004. The 'Rehearsal Room' enables writers to be more proactive in the development of their texts, using audience feedback as a major element of this process. The overall positive responses from the audience and promoters during the drafting and development stage encouraged us to produce this bold new play by Torben Betts. We are delighted to engage some of the most visionary and talented artists to create the world premiere production of *The Unconquered* and are proud to present it as our largest tour to date, touring to 21 venues in Scotland and England, including our first visit to London.

Muriel Romanes
Artistic Director

Acknowledgement

Muriel Romanes at Stellar Quines is perhaps rare these days in that, as an artistic director of a theatre company, she trusts implicitly the skills of the individual writer, affirming that the play which is eventually presented by her company is the writer's responsibility alone and not one that has upon it the signatures of a whole host of collaborators, most of whom are usually not writers at all. This liberating approach takes courage. Both she and her playwrights are highly exposed in this situation – indeed it can be an intimidating experience if productions don't work as well as one might have envisaged. A commission that is more of a co-writing exercise, between playwright and literary department, can create a refuge for the writer should things go wrong. Alone, however, the writer must take all critical responses on the chin, preferably learning to regard both praise and abuse with equal detachment.

Stellar Quines have assisted me in the development of *The Unconquered* by setting up workshops and rehearsed readings at which I have been present. I have largely gauged the development of the play from the enthusiastic commitment and the input of the eight talented actors who took part in the two public readings that were held at the Traverse, in Edinburgh, none of whom are acting in this full production. To all of them I extend my deep gratitude. Not once during the writing of the play have I felt someone peering over my shoulder, so to speak, pressurising me to alter the work. I have been both trusted and respected.

Stellar Quines have given me the time and the space to write exactly the kind of play I want. At the start of the commissioning process I needed give Muriel only the briefest of outlines, since she knows instinctively that plays should always be journeys into the unknown for the dramatist. I have never attempted to write a play quite like this before, indeed I am always looking to take myself out of my own comfort zone, and so *The Unconquered* is something of a risk for me. It is therefore also a risk for this brave and generous theatre company. Given that they are known for working predominantly with Scottish women, it is remarkable that they have commissioned a play from a writer, who is both English and male. The whole experience has been extremely liberating and I am hugely grateful to Muriel Romanes and her company for giving me the opportunity to move myself a little further forward as a dramatist.

I would also like to extend my thanks to James Hogan and Charles Glanville at Oberon Books for their amazing generosity and support throughout my writing career.

Torben Betts, January 2007

Comfort Zone

I can recall the first time that I ever used black India ink. It was at school in Edinburgh. Our teacher, Peter Standen was trying to get us to be more courageous and experimental: '…This stuff is uncompromising…once you make your mark…that's it…no going back.'

Several years ago I had the opportunity to spend some time living and working in Havana. Despite all the dynamic and colour that is Cuban culture, I had real difficulties getting access to any basic art materials. The US trade embargo and the collapse of the Soviet Union had crippled the already fragile Cuban economy. In the event, I managed to find some black India ink and paper and spent the period of my residency producing a new portfolio of drawings, one that reflected my own response to a society and people that has resisted being shaped and influenced by external forces.

The use of black ink to visualise the story of *The Unconquered* seems contextually appropriate from the outset – Torben's introductory text signalled that we should experience the play in a bold, almost comic-book world. The new drawings that have emerged in the studio serve many purposes. They are a transcription of the core themes and a catalyst to the design of the set. Other larger drawings created as part of the rehearsal process have become a physical component part of the dynamic space in which the story unfolds. As with *The Unconquered*, the use of black ink takes us out of our comfort zone. Its unpredictable nature and autonomous properties can often lead to some impressive accidents. The floor of the studio immediately underneath my drawing table frequently takes some direct hits.

I am sure that Mr Standen would approve.

Keith McIntyre

Ducks on a Stormy Lake

The physical world of *The Unconquered* is unbridled and passing, with great alacrity, from order to chaos. The story is told on many levels at once. The words the characters speak are often an attempt to keep the world under control and manageable, but the kinds of things they are forced to do in Torben Betts' imagination often tell us the opposite story. Their previously safe everyday habits are of less and less use to them, and in the face of events become absurdly malformed. On top of this, like a crazy cartoon, the built world of this troubled family leaps into farcical life, forcing the characters into physical behaviour that is decidedly not ordinary. These people are ducks paddling like mad to keep from going under.

A C Wilson

THANK YOU TO

REDDING PARK DEVELOPMENT Company Ltd.

Stellar Quines is delighted to introduce our principal tour sponsor REDDING PARK DEVELOPMENT Company Ltd. to you. Our sponsor is a new sponsor to the arts and shares a common commitment to excellence, sustainability and creative partnerships.

We are immensely grateful for the invaluable support from REDDING PARK DEVELOPMENT which has been match-funded by the 'Scottish Executive New Arts Sponsorship Awards' in conjunction with Arts & Business Scotland, allowing us to reach audiences across the country to a wide geographical and demographic spread.

REDDING PARK DEVELOPMENT is at the forefront in land remediation in Scotland. They acquire contaminated sites and convert them into useful land. The recycled and transformed land can then be used for parkland, housing, leisure or commerce, and therefore making valuable land available for future use.

The company is expanding and developing new land remediation projects across the country and are always on the lookout for new problem sites. Please contact their office for further information on future plans and projects.

Contact details for Redding Park Development:

Gordon Macpherson
Email: gm@gordonmacpherson.com
Telephone: 0131 225 2505

Stellar Quines Theatre Company
30B Grindlay Street
Edinburgh EH3 9AX
Scotland, UK

T: +44 (0)131 248 4836
F: +44 (0)131 228 3955
E: info@stellarquines.co.uk
www.stellarquines.com

Artistic Director Muriel Romanes
General Manager Alexandra Stampler-Brown
Administrator Kirsty Vidler

Board of Directors Lynn Bains, Alan Dawson, Caroline Middleton, Graeme Baillie, Muriel Romanes, Elaine Carmichael, Gordon Macpherson, John Ramage, Katie Bowling.
Associates Jemima Levick, Alexandra Mathie, Gaynor Macfarlane

Stellar Quines Membership

Join Stellar Quines membership scheme and show your support for Scotland's only theatre company dedicated to promoting and developing the work of women in theatre.

Your annual contribution will allow us to continue to commission new ground-breaking, thought-provoking, brave and high quality theatre, to nurture and mentor young theatre practitioners and to tour extensively.

By becoming a Stellar Quines Star, you will play a special role in the work that we do, touring seductive, bold theatre to audiences across Scotland and beyond.

Stellar Quines Star Benefits

- Welcome Pack including Stellar Quines 'Star' badge
- Invitation to attend opening nights with a chance to meet and chat to the cast and crew at post-show receptions
- Invitation to a members event
- Three newsletters per year
- Credit on all print material and website
- The exhilaration of knowing you are instrumental in supporting the women of Scottish Theatre

For more information please call **0131 248 4836** or visits our website **www.stellarquines.com** where you can download a membership form.

Credits

Tour Sponsor
Redding Park Development Co. Ltd

Funders
Scottish Arts Council
'Scottish Executive New Arts Sponsorship Awards' in conjunction with Arts & Business Scotland
Highlands & Islands Enterprise

Stellar Quines Star Members
Graeme & Rachel Baillie
Mike & Jane Ridings
Bridget Stevens
Gordon & Margaret Shiach
Margaret Littlewood
Stella Scott
Katie Bowling
Maureen Beattie
Mary Scott-Macfarlane
Alix Gaffney
Adie Chalmers

We would like to thank:

Stephen Wrentmore, Tom Gardner, Susie Normand, Drew Wallis
and all the staff at the Byre Theatre of St Andrews
Gatti Design
Grays Fabrication Cupar
Pitlochry Festival Theatre

St Andrew's University THEATRE AMBASSADORS:
Emma Corbishley, James Lumsden, Carly Matthews and Kieran Hennigan

Torben Betts
THE UNCONQUERED

with thanks to W Somerset Maugham

First published in 2007 by Oberon Books Ltd.
521 Caledonian Road, London N7 9RH
Tel: 020 7607 3637 / Fax: 020 7607 3629
e-mail: info@oberonbooks.com
www.oberonbooks.com

A catalogue record for this book is available from the British Library.

ISBN: 1 84002 723 1 / 978-1-84002-723-5

Cover illustration by Keith McIntyre.
Design by Gatti.

Printed in Great Britain by Antony Rowe Ltd, Chippenham.

Characters

GIRL

MOTHER

FATHER

SOLDIER

to be played without an interval

Note
The text presented here was correct at the time
of going to press but slight changes have been
made during rehearsals.

for my two boys
Stanley (5) and Leo (1)

Part One

Exordium: the sound of a woman sobbing with a heavy grief. The GIRL, in a school uniform, stands reading. She is appalled by what she reads. She closes the book. The sobbing fades.

GIRL: How I...hate. How I...loathe. How I...abhor.

MOTHER: (*Entering.*) This we know.

GIRL: But now here comes the question...

MOTHER: The question?

GIRL: Has my hatred for this stinking world finally corrupted my capacity for...

MOTHER: ...compassion?

GIRL: Yes.

MOTHER: Possibly.

GIRL: Possibly?

MOTHER: If you ever had one.

GIRL: Oh, Mother, I had compassion... I felt it once fluttering in my heart like a wounded butterfly.

MOTHER: I don't recall.

GIRL: You don't?

MOTHER: Its expression.

GIRL: I was kind to a rabbit, a gerbil.

MOTHER: The actual expression of it.

GIRL: Wept at the odd funeral. The sentimental ceremonies with the cardboard boxes.

MOTHER: You were fond of your rodents perhaps but people you have always shunned.

GIRL: Intelligence always questions...

MOTHER: But your circumstances…

GIRL: …its circumstances.

MOTHER: …have always been…

GIRL: Desires always to experience…

MOTHER: They have always been…

GIRL: …discomfort.

MOTHER: …comfortable.

GIRL: Discontent.

MOTHER: Contented.

GIRL: To square up to the pain.

MOTHER: Secure.

GIRL: To the appalling burden of this life.

MOTHER: Why not even say: cocooned?

GIRL: The agony of human loneliness.

MOTHER: Protected.

GIRL: Oh, this rage, this rage…

MOTHER: It now proclaims itself from every pore of your skin. Your complexion was once a blessed thing, was once a smooth and pure perfection, but now it is cracked and coarse like the knuckles of a butcher. When once the scent of summer meadows trailed you as you glided girlishly from room to room, you seem now to reek of stale tobacco, sweat and barnyard animals. What is more, your decision to waste your life like this, in this limbo of bookishness and solitude, it does not remotely accentuate your feminine charms. Tell me, why does that handsome boy, and oh he had such a voice, the smooth velvet voice of a judge or a fox-hunter, why does he no longer come to call?

GIRL: His lack of anger bored me, his unthinking faith in authority appalled me. He had not excavated his soft and privileged upbringing for a second. His ideology was simply copied from his father: a virtue learned by rote, a manufactured kindness. Oh, his aching wish to do good in the world, to mould it after his own precious morality. In short, Mother, he wanted to become a barrister.

MOTHER: A society needs its lawyers.

GIRL: If only they stuck to the swindle of the law.

MOTHER: But this boy loved you!

GIRL: He wanted my body merely. To rub his mole-marked flesh on mine. To squirt his sadness between my thighs.

MOTHER: He wanted to look after you.

GIRL: I look after myself!

MOTHER: Take you out for decent meals.

GIRL: I grow my own food.

MOTHER: Your ragged vegetable patch?

GIRL: At least applaud the attempt.

MOTHER: You would have wanted for nothing.

GIRL: I will now return to my reading!

MOTHER: And what of the roof over your head?

GIRL: My birthright. The house of my ancestors!

MOTHER: But you are missing out on such a wondrous world.

GIRL: And what would you know of that? A bewildered bride straight from school, your milk-white veil flapping...that proclamation of virginity no doubt the first sham of many...flapping in the autumn wind, the dark skies above the church presaging your lifetime of despair...oh yes, I have seen the photographs...and then a wife, a mother, a domestic drudge...

MOTHER: Your insults I dodge.

GIRL: …suffocating in silent boredom. This nauseating quest for pity, for sympathy!

MOTHER: Your rudeness I reject.

GIRL: Do not address me, sponge! I shall no longer weep for you!

MOTHER: See how I ignore your spiteful, undaughterly words.

GIRL: I shall never live like you.

MOTHER: I said the same to my own mother…

GIRL: And yet your fate…

MOTHER: …has been identical.

GIRL: Yes.

MOTHER: (*Aside.*) I look in the mirror and it is her that I see!

GIRL: (*Taking up the book again.*) There are so many pages…

MOTHER: Such sadness around the eyes.

GIRL: …and so little time.

MOTHER: But you must not barricade yourself away from the world, endlessly flipping pages like this and ranting at the radio.

GIRL: I have lost my innocence.

MOTHER: You berate your father and I for our affectionate yet strangely passionless existence, our stable yet dreary little marriage…

GIRL: It is all just so much…exhalation!

MOTHER: But we must live at peace with the world?

GIRL: Those who affirm they are at peace are perhaps already dead!

MOTHER: To be alive is to choose. And then of course one must adhere to those choices no matter how much misery they bring. These are the responsibilities of love, the agonies of the domestic life. My little routines, which you so mock and so deride, they are what maintain my equanimity. They also enable me to hold up my head in the town and to wear my excellent hats.

GIRL: And thus you blot out the slaughter beyond your window!

MOTHER: As you evade reality with all your...alco-booze.

GIRL: I cannot take any more of this!

MOTHER: And it is nice to eat at regular hours.

GIRL: I shall read my way out of this tedium.

MOTHER: It assists the digestion.

GIRL: I shall hate and curse until my days are done.

MOTHER: And so, accordingly, I have prepared yet another wholesome casserole.

GIRL: Your tone, Mother, always so conciliatory, always so infuriatingly... (*A long pause as she chooses.*) ...calm.

MOTHER: You must look at things more simply. You are safe here. The climate is temperate. Enjoy your youth. (*She stifles a sob.*) I, with such a baffled ingratitude, threw mine away.

GIRL: What possible good is this god of family when it always becomes this, this...fortress of idiocy?!!

MOTHER: We have this discussion every day.

GIRL: Yes! Even this, the outpourings of my tormented soul, the lamentations of my screaming heart, even all this seems to follow a pattern!

Enter the FATHER *in his suit, a newspaper open, reading. He walks centre stage.*

The women watch him.

MOTHER: Speak then. Won't you speak? Please. Tell us. What is happening in the world.

FATHER: It is quite extraordinary.

MOTHER: It is?

FATHER: The Government has been brought down. Millions in the cities have stormed the buildings. It is a people's revolution.

GIRL: I knew nothing of this.

FATHER: Our leaders have been cast onto the streets and pelted with excrement.

GIRL: Let them be slaughtered! Let them all be drowned in the muddy river!

FATHER: Our humdrum way of life…will suffer, will… (*A pause as he chooses.*) …change.

MOTHER: But…your salary, the money on the twenty-sixth of each month!?

FATHER: Regular as clockwork.

FATHER/MOTHER: Oiling the wheels of our modest machine.

GIRL: (*Aside.*) I have so turned my back from the world, so immersed myself in the escapism of fiction and history, that this popular uprising, which might have lent my life meaning, has occurred completely without me!

FATHER: This is extraordinary. The police force and the army have sided with the public and refused to obey orders. Senior figures of the Government have been imprisoned and charged with war crimes. Our secretive and elitist governance system is to be radically overhauled.

GIRL: This is the greatest of days!

FATHER: A Socialist Republic is now declared, the Monarchy abolished.

GIRL: How I applaud!

FATHER: All religion is to be removed from public life, all industry to be nationalised.

GIRL: How I celebrate!

FATHER: Public welfare is to be placed, it seems, above private advantage.

GIRL: How I rejoice!

FATHER: But wait. They were controlling interest rates so expertly. The equity in this house. It is our security. And what of the stockmarket?

GIRL: Let it come down, Father! Let it all come down!

FATHER: It is easy for you to be so fearless. You have no property, no family. We, who have invested so heavily in the...

GIRL: Such a droning liberal, such a knee-rubber, such a head-shaker, such a tutt-tutt-tutter! Such shuffling self-hatred!

FATHER: I cannot take on board all these events on an empty stomach. Let me eat and then I shall give you my view of the situation. And please do remember that I shall brook no contradiction.

The sound of his eating fills the stage. Then:

What has happened today in the wider world is indeed extraordinary. The general public has finally stirred from its semi-conscious state and taken action. In many ways this is a good thing since dissent and criticism are essential to the flourishing of a healthy democracy...

GIRL: This is a sham democracy!

FATHER: If you would allow me to finish?

GIRL: Today the light of Truth has dawned upon our sorry land!

MOTHER: Do allow him to finish! It will make life easier for me.

FATHER: However, it seems certain that the Free World will not simply stand back and let everyday people administer their own countries and make political decisions for themselves. I suspect that there will be a reaction to this…one hesitates to say the word…revolution. And this reaction might well be rather unpleasant. Incidentally this latest casserole is quite extraordinary.

GIRL: Oh, you Liberal, you Bourgeois, you Wicketkeeper!

MOTHER weeps.

FATHER: You have made your mother cry.

GIRL: She always cries.

MOTHER: (*Through her tears.*) Not always. You exaggerate.

GIRL: Then often.

MOTHER: I simply want us to be a happy family. It is my life's undertaking!

FATHER: Do not make your mother cry. (*To MOTHER.*) Incidentally, do I here detect a subtle hint of dill?

GIRL: Why are you so sure it was me?

FATHER: It has always been, as you know, one of my favourite herbs.

GIRL: That made her cry?

MOTHER: (*With an effort.*) I am crying because…

FATHER: She is crying because…

GIRL: Let her answer!

FATHER: Do not adopt that...

GIRL: Surely she knows...

FATHER: ...sneering...

GIRL: ...the roots of her own...

FATHER: ...and disrespectful tone...

GIRL: ...emotions...

FATHER: ...with me.

GIRL: ...as well as, if not better than, you.

FATHER: Your own father.

GIRL: And anyway...it is too late.

MOTHER: I am crying because...

GIRL: Because she is already crying.

FATHER: And I am not a liberal.

GIRL: One day you will say something from the heart, a truth forced raw and screeching from the howling depths of your soul.

FATHER: You have no respect for me.

GIRL: Oh, I have wasted my time in this place.

FATHER: Or your mother.

GIRL: I shall throw my lot in with my countrymen. With the concerned academics, those furrow-browed lecturers, as well as with the bloated, belligerent beer-swiggers of these islands.

FATHER: Extraordinary.

GIRL: I shall seek out my own suicide, fighting to preserve this most noble of enterprises!

MOTHER: (*Through tears.*) You must continue with your education.

GIRL: The classroom leads always to the office, the pension. We are none of us born for four walls and a desk!

FATHER: You will go back to the school. Your intelligence was prized highly by the professor there…

GIRL: That meths-swilling testicle scratcher! That bearded arse stench! No! I need a cause. And this shall be it!

FATHER studies the paper again as:

MOTHER: I beg you!

GIRL: My mind is made up.

MOTHER: I beg you to reconsider!

GIRL: I shall write.

FATHER: (*Behind his paper.*) Quite extraordinary.

MOTHER: But what will I do without you?

GIRL: Live your life.

MOTHER: But I don't want to. I hate it!

GIRL: I cannot be responsible.

FATHER: (*Behind his paper.*) Quite extraordinary.

MOTHER: Please, tell me what to do.

GIRL: Learn to love the life you've chosen.

MOTHER: I have tried but I cannot.

GIRL: Then leave.

MOTHER: But I have my duty!

GIRL: Then stay.

FATHER: (*Behind his paper.*) Quite extraordinary.

MOTHER: But just he and I alone in these rooms!?

GIRL: Then leave.

MOTHER: But he is my husband. I cannot just leave him!

GIRL: Then stay.

MOTHER: But the loneliness, the boredom, the unending circularities!

GIRL: Then leave.

MOTHER: What are you saying? Life isn't so simple.

GIRL: Then stay.

MOTHER: But it's been for you that I have lived. You, my precious child. Not this pompous dullard who shares my bed.

GIRL: Then leave.

MOTHER: Be serious. I took an oath when I married.

GIRL: Then stay.

FATHER: (*Behind his paper.*) Quite extraordinary.

MOTHER: I cannot face this soul-searing solitude!

FATHER: This could be civil war.

GIRL: And on whose side will you be fighting?

MOTHER: Why all this talk of fighting?

GIRL: No change ever came if not through the spilling of blood.

MOTHER: Up until minutes ago I was happily preparing a wholesome casserole, as I have done for decades at around this time, and now it is all fighting and bloodshed and revolution! Whatever happened to the peaceful life?

GIRL: It must be fought for. There must be struggle.

MOTHER/FATHER: Oh, for goodness sake, will you please be
    nice!

GIRL: I spit on your nice. I shit on your nice.

FATHER: (*Suddenly standing.*) We must bury our belongings!
    Save our possessions from the envious hoards! Where is
    your jewellery?

MOTHER: My jewellery?

GIRL: Your niceness is surely…

FATHER: We must conceal our treasured items.

GIRL: Your niceness is surely…

MOTHER: Muddy my bangles, my pendants, my rings? These
    are close to my heart. (*Aside.*) I like to finger them at night.

GIRL: Is surely a symptom of your acquiescence!

FATHER: I must phone the broker, the doctor. Speak to the
    heavy-bellied banker. Contact the accountant!

GIRL: How the ground shakes beneath your feet!

FATHER: We have accumulated!

GIRL: Yes.

FATHER: Accrued and amassed.

GIRL: So as to…?

FATHER: So as to…

GIRL: So as to…?

FATHER: So as to…

GIRL: And what of your pension scheme now?

FATHER: You scoff!

GIRL: I scoff! I jeer! I mock! I sneer!

FATHER: You scoff and yet…

GIRL: When I am your age?

FATHER: Yes.

GIRL: I shall not marry, I shall not… (*A long pause as she chooses.*) …replicate.

MOTHER: But one feels such emptiness as one ages.

GIRL: So you fill up your lives with nappies and daytrips? The arrogance of it all! And then you demand gratitude!

MOTHER: You have been my…achievement.

GIRL: And what an achievement!

MOTHER: To be a parent is a sacred task.

GIRL: It is immoral. Irresponsible.

MOTHER/FATHER: You child, you child…

GIRL: You heave out these infants, you backpat and beam. You gurgle and fawn, how you all sing-song-sing…

MOTHER/FATHER: But what could we do?

GIRL: …as the world burns around you…

MOTHER/FATHER: But what could we do?

GIRL: It's your children who then have to battle the blaze!

MOTHER: We are agreeable people?

FATHER: You have had a good education.

MOTHER: And the odd beach holiday.

FATHER: Excursions, clothes, dolls as a child.

MOTHER: We read to you in your bunk.

FATHER: Bought you ice cream.

MOTHER: And we have visited museums.

FATHER: We are well-respected in the town.

MOTHER: We have good friends.

FATHER: Not intimate perhaps.

MOTHER: But they help pass the time.

FATHER: Not intimate, no.

MOTHER: We play cards together. Board games.

FATHER: And have drinks and parties.

MOTHER: We cook tasty dinners for other couples, of a similar age and background.

FATHER: Who share our middle-class aspirations.

MOTHER: Solid, traditional fare.

FATHER: Who are not ashamed to own stocks and shares.

MOTHER: We compare the careers of our children.

FATHER: And holiday together.

MOTHER: As a welcome respite…

MOTHER/FATHER: From each other.

MOTHER: They are couples who, like us, feel excluded from the world.

FATHER: The promise of our salad days unfulfilled.

MOTHER: They sometimes bring the dessert.

FATHER: We have barbecues out the back.

GIRL: The system you have all profited from and which has given you these things, these untroubled ways of wasting your days, that is what has made me like this. I have been breathing in its rancid air for too long, listening to its lies every day, to the gut-churning hypocrisy, the moral cowardice of its sniggering servants. These ever-so-concerned Christian men, these ever-so-sensible Christian women with their ever-so-sensible Christian hair, these whining apologists for violence, for monarchy! I would joyfully see them all crucified against the whitewashed walls of their Tuscan farmhouses. I would join the long, long queue to help bang in the nails. I see it now: a landscape of lawyers, a swathe of solicitors, a panorama of public servants, all in their Savile Row suits, their wrists ripped and bleeding, their arms outstretched, moaning in pain, their grins turned to grimaces. Their pasty white bellies bursting from their freshly-laundered shirts. The scuffed black briefcases opened at their feet, documents blowing about in the gentle Italian breeze. These arms-dealers, these tobacco-pushers, these twisted moralists, these middle-aged murderers! The huge family cars parked silently on the gravelled drives, brand new metal glinting in the baking sun, the cicadas clicking from the olive trees, their oblivious partners preparing pasta in the red-tiled kitchen with the cobwebbed, wooden beams. Their bandy-legged adolescents splashing in the swimming pool as Daddy writhes and as Mummy chokes. Oh, my senses are corrupted with it, my heart is heavy with it, my fingernails have been chewed to the quick. As a result I am in all probability... (*A long pause as she chooses.*) ...an alcoholic!

FATHER: Then you should have gone out there and helped to change matters!

GIRL: Oh, where is the rage, Father?

MOTHER: Yes, what did you do?

GIRL: Where is the outrage?

FATHER: To help bring down the regime?

GIRL: I... (*A long pause as she chooses.*) ...hated. That is what I have done.

FATHER: (*Aside to MOTHER.*) She is clearly unaware...

MOTHER: (*Aside to FATHER.*) Unaware.

FATHER: (*Aside.*) ...of the complexity of the issues.

MOTHER: (*Aside.*) The complexities...

FATHER: (*Aside.*) Her polemic is too militant.

MOTHER: (*Aside.*) Too militant...

FATHER: (*Aside.*) She should come at her subject more obliquely.

MOTHER: (*Aside.*) Obliquely, yes...

FATHER: (*Aside.*) This is nothing more than an extended rant.

MOTHER: (*Aside.*) The rant is extended and...

FATHER: (*Aside.*) She should add a little humour, humanity to her venom.

MOTHER: (*Aside.*) If her venom was...

FATHER: (*Aside.*) Soften the harshness of her verbal blows.

MOTHER: (*Aside.*) Too harsh, too harsh...

FATHER: (*Aside.*) Win her audience back with some wit.

MOTHER: (*Aside.*) I love a little wit...

FATHER: (*Aside.*) These endless diatribes.

MOTHER: (*Aside.*) Are endless, yes...

FATHER: (*Aside.*) They are without end.

MOTHER: (*Aside.*) I so agree.

GIRL: Stop your gibbering. It is time for the news.

A light change.

A radio crackles. A voice shouts through a megaphone at a cheering and jubilant crowd.

VOICE: My country, I applaud you!

Loud, joyous cheering, whistles, drums etc.

Today must surely be the greatest day in the history of our nation!

Loud, joyous cheering, whistles, drums etc. The speech continues inaudibly. Over this:

MOTHER: Who do these people think they are?

FATHER: Extremists.

MOTHER: Ranting and raging.

FATHER: Life's vicissitudes…I tremble before them.

MOTHER: And I quiver, I quake.

FATHER/MOTHER: The system was not perfect but it suited most of us.

MOTHER: And now everything is uncertain.

FATHER: This is quite extraordinary.

MOTHER: And now everything is uncertain.

FATHER: This is quite extraordinary.

MOTHER: And now everything is uncertain.

FATHER: (*Suddenly standing.*) We must bury our belongings!

MOTHER: And now everything is…

FATHER: Save our possessions from the envious hoards!

MOTHER: …uncertain.

On the radio loud, joyous cheering, whistles, drums etc.

VOICE: …and our ways shall be peaceful, democratic and true. Yes, this is a mandate for real change. And this time…this time you shall not be betrayed! My country, I applaud you!

Loud, joyous cheering, whistles, drums etc.

FATHER: Quite extraordinary.

A loud firework close by. Colours flash across the stage. Cheering.

GIRL: (*Aside.*) I feel strangely excluded. Why am I not among the crowds, chanting and celebrating?

MOTHER: There are people out in the street, look!

FATHER: People?

MOTHER: Out in the street.

MOTHER and FATHER go to a window and look out.

There is Mr Flapjack, the fishmonger. He is punching the air!

FATHER: His bloodied apron still wrapped round his waist.

MOTHER: Brandishing in his fist what looks like a large rainbow trout.

FATHER: Even the trout seems to be smiling.

GIRL: (*Aside.*) My head has been in the sand.

MOTHER: Mrs Tuckshop, the local councillor, she too is leaping about in a delirium of celebration!

FATHER: Her handbag, that so simulates crocodile skin, banging against her bony hip.

MOTHER: A bottle of German lager in her hand.

FATHER: You can see it is German?

MOTHER: I know all the labels.

FATHER: David and Sheila I see...

MOTHER: Dancing in the fountain.

FATHER: See how they embrace as the cherubim of stone pisses water onto their greying hair.

MOTHER: But she ordinarily uses a dye.

GIRL: (*Aside.*) My rage has been ineffective.

MOTHER: Richard and Caroline!

FATHER: They bellow like cattle...

MOTHER: Like cattle, like cattle...

FATHER: They bellow like cattle!

MOTHER: Like cattle they do!

FATHER: So happy...so happy...

MOTHER: So happy...so happy...

FATHER: So happy...so happy...

MOTHER: So happy they are...

GIRL: (*Aside.*) I have been directionless.

FATHER: Harry and Margaret.

MOTHER: Arms round the shoulders...

FATHER: Of their strapping young sons!

MOTHER: That self-absorbed postman...

FATHER: With the straggly beard.

MOTHER: On his unroadworthy bicycle.

FATHER: Riding in circles.

MOTHER: A figure of eight surely?

FATHER: ...like he was handicapped.

MOTHER: That waiter from Alfredo's...

FATHER: The Italian boy...

MOTHER: A flag draped around his well-muscled body.

FATHER: Or is it a tablecloth?

MOTHER: I would venture a flag.

FATHER: Red, white and green.

MOTHER: This is truly an international spate of revelry.

GIRL: (*Aside.*) Today, yes, I come of age.

FATHER: That girl from the chemist's!

MOTHER: The Albino.

GIRL: (*Aside.*) And I change my life forever.

FATHER: Sat high on the shoulders of lecherous Fred.

MOTHER: The landlord of the Old Red Lion.

FATHER: He is clasping her bare, white thighs in his large, red and blistered hands.

GIRL: (*Aside.*) And yet when I join up with my comrades I must be fully informed.

The GIRL picks up her book and begins reading again.

MOTHER: The vicar with the poor eyesight.

FATHER: The Indian doctor and his whole family.

MOTHER: The builder with the breath.

FATHER: The baker who is bent.

MOTHER: The beggar with the bandaged body.

MOTHER/FATHER: The town has never seemed so alive.

A loud firework close by. Colours flash across the stage. Cheering.

FATHER: Change terrifies me. And yet my tragedy is this: the thought of my life remaining on its present course forever, this monotonous cycle of cereal breakfasts and black coffee, of mouse-clicking and keyboard-tapping, of tired meetings and tittle-tattle, of daily papers and silent evenings…the thought that things shall be always like this until, at the end of such an unlived life, I stumble wearily into my damp and desolate grave, oh this thought sends shudders of horror through my whole being.

MOTHER: You were fearless when younger.

FATHER: A disguise adopted to convince my father I could make something of myself.

MOTHER: Make your way in the world.

FATHER: Inside I was trembling.

MOTHER: Each sunrise a curse.

FATHER: Each sunset a relief.

MOTHER: And yet your youthful swagger?

FATHER: The pressure to succeed.

MOTHER: You excelled as a cricketer.

FATHER: If only I were a boy again.

MOTHER: Yet you were thrashed?

FATHER: Mercilessly.

MOTHER: For any falling-off of standards.

FATHER: The grades at school, the examinations, oh!

MOTHER: Yours was a preordained life.

FATHER: Preordained to be ordinary.

MOTHER: A mindless automaton.

FATHER: A hamster in its wheel.

MOTHER: A muncher of mass-produced meat.

FATHER: I have simply gone through the motions of a life.

MOTHER: Yet there is love. Simple love.

FATHER: Have we loved?

MOTHER: Have we…?

FATHER: Can you tell me that you love me?

She does not respond at first.

MOTHER: With my hand on my heart…

FATHER: You can tell me…?

MOTHER: That I love you. Yes.

FATHER: You cast down your eyes.

MOTHER: Did I?

FATHER: When you said it?

MOTHER: I do. Love you. Yes. I do.

FATHER: Have I made you happy?

She does not respond at first.

MOTHER: With my hand on my heart…

FATHER: You can tell me…?

MOTHER: That you have made me happy. Yes.

FATHER: You cast down your eyes.

MOTHER: Did I?

FATHER: When you said it?

MOTHER: You have. Made me happy. Happy. You have.

FATHER: Then it appears that I had better hold you.

MOTHER: Hold me?

He goes to her. He stands before her awkwardly.

FATHER: I am going to hold you now.

MOTHER: Yes.

FATHER: Going to hold you.

MOTHER: You said.

FATHER: We must keep out the cold.

MOTHER: The coming storm.

They do not move.

FATHER: I am going to hold you now.

MOTHER: You said.

FATHER: Then kindly step forward.

She steps forward. He slowly puts his arms around her.

They stand in that pose in a stiff awkwardness.

After a time.

Does that help at all?

MOTHER: Oh yes. Oh yes, it really really does.

The GIRL suddenly flinches at something she reads. Her hand covers her mouth.

As the FATHER and MOTHER continue to hold onto one another, the sound of the woman sobbing returns.

Part Two

The very loud sound of jet aircraft overhead. Massive explosions. MOTHER and FATHER, newspaper open. Neither speak for some time. They have to shout above the noise.

MOTHER: Speak then! Won't you speak?! Tell us! What is happening! In the world!

FATHER: It is quite extraordinary!

MOTHER: It is?!

FATHER: The editor beseeches us to surrender immediately! Says this revolution cannot be sustained! Says that remaining independent will be disastrous in the long-term! Says the country will be unable to feed itself!

MOTHER: How I want all this bombing to stop!

FATHER: Says that we cannot be held to ransom by a few extremists!

MOTHER: One cannot squat in a cellar!

FATHER: Who seek to destroy our way of life forever!

MOTHER: Indefinitely!

FATHER: Says we must release the Prime Minister!

MOTHER: It so restricts one's movements!

FATHER: And restore him to power!

MOTHER: One's freedoms!

FATHER: His rightful position!

MOTHER: And we must live on what we grow from the ground!?

FATHER: Before he's restored for us!

MOTHER: One cannot live on root vegetables!

FATHER: Before more lives are lost!

MOTHER: Indefinitely!

FATHER: The Free World will not tolerate governments with unconventional philosophies!

MOTHER: I would like a little pâté!

FATHER: Opposition will not be allowed!

MOTHER: From time to time!

FATHER: There is no alternative to the Free World!

MOTHER: I have been brought up to expect…

FATHER: We must all grow up and see!

MOTHER: …just a little luxury!

FATHER: This incontrovertible truth!

MOTHER: Just a little comfort!

FATHER: And yet most of the population seem keen to resist!

MOTHER: And why bomb us?

FATHER: They want to change the way we're governed!

MOTHER: Why bomb our nice little town?

FATHER: To decentralise!

MOTHER: Our pretty squares, our peaceful parks…

FATHER: To put power back in the hands of the ordinary man!

MOTHER: The statue of the monarch!

FATHER: The ordinary woman!

MOTHER: As she sits side-saddle…

FATHER: And away from the corporations!

MOTHER: On her strong silver steed!

FATHER: So one can only surmise that the newspapers and the broadcast media…

MOTHER: Yes, why don't they just bomb the cities?

FATHER: …do not reflect public opinion!

MOTHER: Perhaps it's to weaken our morale!

FATHER: These people are our allies!

MOTHER: But I have no morale!

FATHER: Our brothers in arms!

MOTHER: I'm not sleeping at night!

FATHER: Our friends, our protectors!

MOTHER: Let us just say we are sorry!

FATHER: But it seems they do not want us…

MOTHER: Go back to how it used to be!

FATHER: …to be an example to others!

MOTHER: The system was not perfect!

FATHER: We could spread this…

MOTHER: But it suited most of us!

FATHER: …this virus of independence!

MOTHER: And now everything is uncertain!

The sound of a jet aircraft overhead.

Numerous white leaflets now flutter down upon the stage.

MOTHER and FATHER eye each other nervously.

MOTHER bends down and gathers some up.

She is about to read one when FATHER, a Hardy to her Laurel, clicks his fingers.

She obediently passes the leaflets to him. He reads.

Speak then. Won't you speak? Please. Tell us. What is happening. In the world.

FATHER: It is quite extraordinary.

MOTHER: It is?

He picks up a leaflet and reads.

FATHER: 'We urge you, the people of a once-proud nation, to surrender immediately.'

He reads another leaflet.

'This revolution cannot be sustained.'

He reads another leaflet.

'Remaining independent will be disastrous in the long-term.'

He reads another leaflet.

'Continuing sanctions will mean you will be unable to feed yourselves.'

He reads another leaflet.

'You are decent, law-abiding people who, like us, love freedom. You cannot be held to ransom by a few extremists, who seek to destroy your way of life forever.'

He reads another leaflet.

'You must release the Prime Minister. And restore him to power. He is not a war criminal. He is a good, Christian man.'

He drops the leaflet.

Let me give you my overview. Let me give you my… summing up.

MOTHER: Yes?

FATHER: It is inconceivable, that a full-scale invasion of this country will ever actually take place. We are the land from which their ancestors sprung. We have only to wait for those of us who oppose this sudden change in government to reorganise ourselves, for the soldiers and the police force of this land to rejoin their former employers, to break the cabinet members out of their cells, to swear allegiance once more to the crown and to the state and all will be well. No. There is no reason at all to fear.

Suddenly massive gunfire very close by. Shouts, screams. Machine guns. Explosions.

The GIRL rushes on, in combat gear.

GIRL: They are here! The enemy! In the town!

More gunfire and shouts. The sound of helicopters overhead.

FATHER/MOTHER: Our liberators?

GIRL: The invaders!

FATHER/MOTHER: Our liberators?

GIRL: Your gaolers!

FATHER/MOTHER: The system was not perfect but it suited most of us.

GIRL: (*Handing him a large, serrated knife.*) Each citizen is being given a weapon. The gangs, the drug-pushers, the aimless youth of the country are pooling their tools. Crack dealers with crew-cuts are out on the streets happily handing over their sawn-off shotguns to the previously timid and deskbound. The criminals are uniting with the godfearing. Here, Mother. For you. (*She hands her a similar knife.*) We have this also. (*She shows them a revolver.*) I shall keep it since I do not believe your feeble hearts are wholly in this revolution.

MOTHER: What am I to do with this?

GIRL: Defend yourself.

MOTHER: The only knives I use are for cutting a loaf, for dicing carrots or for finely slicing those large and unwieldy beefheart tomatoes.

FATHER: Beef*steak* tomatoes.

MOTHER: Is that what they call them?

FATHER: Beef*steak* tomatoes, yes.

MOTHER: Beefsteak tomatoes.

FATHER: But I bought you that slicing machine?

MOTHER: I just prefer to use a knife.

FATHER: But I bought you that slicing machine?

MOTHER: I simply prefer to use a knife.

FATHER: (*Angry.*) Did I, or did I not, buy you that very expensive slicing machine!?

GIRL: Here…defend yourself from the Free World.

MOTHER: You have gone quite mad.

GIRL: Even if we are obliterated those who come after us will look back and see just how close we came.

MOTHER: But I do not wish to be…

GIRL: They will be proud of us.

MOTHER: …obliterated.

GIRL: We shall be an example to them all.

FATHER: And I do not like my daughter carrying armaments. Of any description.

Heavy explosions and machine-gun fire continue throughout.

GIRL: Our senses have been dulled by the banal thuds of popular music, we have been distracted by so much soap opera and celebrity. Let us build up a bonfire and burn all the boybands! Let us gnaw at the bones of those who would entertain!

MOTHER: We were brought up to be pacifists.

GIRL: How these comedians presume…

FATHER: To repudiate violence.

GIRL: How these entertainers presume…

MOTHER: My father was President of the Local Pacifist Society.

FATHER: It was *my* father who held that particular honour…

GIRL: These backslappers, these joke tellers…

MOTHER: If I may correct you…

GIRL: How they presume that their infantile observations…

FATHER: Your father was only Vice-President…

GIRL: …will somehow lighten our darkness.

FATHER: …and was Acting President for a period of just seven weeks when my father was taken sick with…

MOTHER: The clap.

FATHER: It was not the clap…

MOTHER: The people in the town maintain…

FATHER: That is defamation.

MOTHER: Your father was a violent man.

FATHER: His temper would on occasion flare up but his was a peaceable nature at root.

MOTHER: And yet he thrashed you?

FATHER: Mercilessly.

MOTHER: And your mother?

FATHER: Her he did not thrash.

MOTHER: I always understood that…

FATHER: On her he would use his fists.

MOTHER: I see.

The GIRL practises with the gun.

Massive explosions throughout this:

FATHER: To thrash is to beat soundly, severely, usually with
the aid of an implement of some nature. It implies, does
it not, that a form of discipline is being meted out? Some
form of moral correction? As a headmaster thrashes
an unruly pupil, or the captain of some ancient bark
thrashes an unsuccessful mutineer or a sailor guilty of
insubordination. And this was indeed the case as far
as my own suffering went. A failed exam at school, a
prolonged spate of bedwetting, a sock left discarded on
the bedroom floor, an inclination to question his authority
or even his opinion. For this was I summoned into his
study and furiously thrashed. With a belt, with a cane,
with a Wellington boot. My buttocks accordingly became
a veritable latticework of weals and abscesses. To this day I
am scarred physically.

MOTHER: And mentally.

FATHER: Whereas with her he would simply lash out. A
word out of place, a meal over-cooked, or even just for
the sheer release of it, when the nightmare of his working
life, the aching sense of failure and worthlessness that
dogged him to the end, in tandem with a weakness for malt
whisky, would explode into a vicious orgy of punches and
headbutts. My mother, as you will remember, was often to
be seen haunting the charity shops…

MOTHER: …in her unquenchable thirst for second-hand
clothing…

FATHER: ...sporting a large pair of sunglasses, with her arm in a sling.

MOTHER: He was a good President, though. In his way.

FATHER: This violence was in the main a reaction to his time in the armed forces.

MOTHER: And you have never struck me.

FATHER: I exercise extreme self-control...

The sound of a door being kicked off its hinges. The sounds of street-fighting increase in volume.

The SOLDIER, in military gear, comes on, pointing a large combat rifle at the family.

SOLDIER: There's some old git out there, right, must be over a hundred years of age, string vest, handkerchief around his baldin' wrinkled head and he's comin' at me ragin', swingin' this big fuckin' garden rake!

MOTHER: Oh, the language, the language...

FATHER: We object to the language!

SOLDIER: And he's climbin' over the wall of his little 'ouse, right, tramplin' on his own geraniums, on his prize fuckin' roses, and then he's screamin' bloody murder at me! Can see right down into his fuckin' throat, his fuckin' gums flappin' about, wavin' this rusty fuckin' rake around like it's a fuckin' flamethrower. I mean I don't wanna gun this old feller down, do I, someone's fuckin' Grandpapa... I don't wanna gun 'im down but what do yer fuckin' do?

MOTHER: Oh, the language, the language...

FATHER: We object to the language.

GIRL: Get out of this house!

SOLDIER: But I don't wanna be fuckin' scraped neither, do I? I don't wanna be fuckin' scraped and get fuckin' rust poisonin'. So he's right up close to me and he's swingin' this fuckin' rake right at me. I'm duckin' and dodgin' like some middleweight fighter, bobbin' and weavin' and toin' and froin' and then he howls something about the Grenadier Guards, when men were men, 'e goes. I'm a soldier of the Free fuckin' World I tell 'im and I don't want no fuckin' history lesson, thank you very much.

MOTHER: Oh, the language, the language…

FATHER: We object to the language.

SOLDIER: So then he only goes and scrapes me. With the rake. Then 'e tries to knock me fuckin' helmet off. I'm clearly peeved at this so I fire a few rounds into his bony white legs, I mean we're talkin' about a bloke who fights in shorts and fuckin' sandals, right, and then I leave him there sprawlin' about, utterin' the sort of expletives yer don't normally associate with a man in his dotage.

GIRL: Get out of this house!

SOLDIER: And then, possibly as a reprisal for this violent deed of mine, I get some Asian geezer takin' fuckin' pot shots at me with a fuckin' Kalishnokov. From above the newsagents out there. Union Jack hangin' from his window, hatred and defiance pouring from his seethin' gob. And so I take him out easy, his bearded little head burstin' apart like a fuckin' watermelon! But I tell yer what…we WILL secure this town! Nasty-lookin' knife yer got there!

FATHER: It's not mine!

SOLDIER: As I say we have a situation where we got a lotta untrained civilian types carryin' round whole arsenals of highly dangerous kit. And if yer don't know what you're doin' yer gonna cut yerself up good and proper. Jus' seen some Women's Institute-type in a purple frock take off the top of her skull with an assault rifle that went outta commission quite some fuckin' time ago.

MOTHER: Oh, the language, the language…

FATHER: We object to the language.

GIRL: Get out of this house!

SOLDIER: Just keep that gun pointin' at the floor!

MOTHER/FATHER: We are meek and law-abiding citizens who love freedom.

SOLDIER: My old man used to tell us the meek shall inherit the earth. He was a religious man but he was also a fightin' man, a killin' man, a slaughterin' man. From a long line o' fightin' and killin' and slaughterin' men. S'in the blood. Shootin' folk to me came in with the mother's milk. Would you mind droppin' your weapons at all?

The FATHER throws down his knife and holds up his hands.

GIRL: Your cowardice is beyond…

FATHER: We have to be practical.

SOLDIER: Now I'd like some booze, if you'd be so kind. To numb the pain of all this murderin' I'm currently engaged in. Drop your weapon, Madam, please.

The MOTHER drops her knife and holds up her hands.

GIRL: Your cowardice is beyond…

MOTHER: We have to be practical.

SOLDIER: And I don't much like the life but when a man gets to a certain age it's 'ard for him to change. This is my career. It follows a path, right. It gives my days…a structure.

FATHER: I can empathise with that. My retirement, when it comes, is something I dread.

SOLDIER: All that time. All that fuckin' freedom.

MOTHER: Oh the language, the language…

FATHER: We object to the language.

SOLDIER: Could give a man the fear.

FATHER: I so need to work. And not just for the money. I hold onto the tedious routine of it all as a drowning man clutches a piece of floating timber.

SOLDIER: Yer not had to kill though? Yer not had to stop a man's heart from beatin', his lungs from breathin', just because he looked at yer a bit funny-like? Never had to break a mother's heart with one nervous contraction of an index finger, safe in the anonymity of the uniform yer wear?

FATHER: We're not really in that line, no.

SOLDIER: Yer done alright then. Yer got a nice enough 'ouse. A nice little family. Your Vauxhall Cavalier was quite a model in its day, though now of course it's riddled with bullet holes. Also...your daughter's got spirit. I'm rather taken with her, truth to tell.

GIRL: Rot in hell.

FATHER: But I have sat on the same chair, at the same desk, facing the same wall, in the same...

SOLDIER: So let's all get drunk, shall we? And I miss a bitta female company. I'm quite lonely really. Sometimes I could do with a nice spot of motherin'.

GIRL: You came to the wrong place.

SOLDIER: Me 'ead lyin' gently on a female breast, me achin' temples soothed by slim fingers, inhalin' some exotic perfume, legs entwined, skin to skin like.

GIRL: Keep it to yourself.

SOLDIER: Sometimes I dream of doin' the old commutin' bit. Get on the chuff-chuff of a mornin', see the glorious green countryside through the scratched-up plastic, sit me tired arse on a piece of upholstery or at worst be forced to stand up, chest to chest like, with the rest of the fuckin' clockwatchers.

MOTHER: Oh the language, the language…

FATHER: We object to the language.

SOLDIER: I'd know where I was. Have a wife to go home to maybes.

MOTHER: My husband's salary… it's paid in on the twenty-sixth of each month.

FATHER: Regular as clockwork.

FATHER/MOTHER: Oiling the wheels of our modest machine.

SOLDIER: Am I making yer nervous?

MOTHER: A little, yes.

SOLDIER: I get a bit melancholic when confronted with such a blissful domestic scene as this.

FATHER/MOTHER: But we are thoroughly dysfunctional.

SOLDIER: Sometimes I just wanna wipe it all out.

FATHER: I quite understand.

SOLDIER: Spray a few rounds, take a few fuckin' seconds…

MOTHER: Oh the language, the language…

FATHER: We object to the language.

SOLDIER: …all three of yer drop like stones.

FATHER: Perhaps some wine then?

SOLDIER: I'd like to relax my grip on this though. I been holding this hunk of metal in this position for quite some fuckin' time now.

MOTHER: Oh the language, the language…

FATHER: We object to the language.

SOLDIER: I imagine a log fire cracklin', the red of the wine minglin' with the deep orange of the flame, a grandfather clock tickin' quietly, the backdrop to some idyllic, ordered world, me weary legs rested up on a leather pouffe. Hard to enjoy the pleasures of the grape when yer wieldin' a great brute like this, isn't it?

MOTHER: (*To the GIRL.*) Won't you please put your gun down?

GIRL: Not while there is breath in my body.

FATHER: He is a professional soldier and you are just a silly little schoolgirl.

MOTHER: He is a very nice man and he's being extremely patient.

FATHER: You must show some respect.

SOLDIER: Important to show respect to your folks. My father was a nasty bastard but I respected 'im nonetheless.

FATHER: I believe that you and I have a lot in common.

SOLDIER: Your pa a tad brutish?

FATHER: Oh yes.

SOLDIER: But yer needed his approval?

FATHER: Oh yes.

SOLDIER: Despite what he did to yer mother?

FATHER: Oh yes.

SOLDIER: And to you, that shivering little shrimp in short trousers?

FATHER: Oh yes.

SOLDIER: Well, another time and another place we could go to the boozer together and swap the sad, sad stories of our formative years.

The SOLDIER momentarily drifts off into reverie and the GIRL suddenly kicks him hard in the groin. He buckles over.

As she turns to point her gun at him, he springs up and points his at her again.

They stand opposite each other, breathing heavily, guns ready to fire. They begin to circle one another.

A helicopter overhead.

Posh totty!

GIRL: Filthy lout!

SOLDIER: You snout-in-the-air pony-rider!

GIRL: You trigger-happy tabloid-reader!

SOLDIER: You latte-drinker, you pampered princess!

GIRL: You brainless order-obeyer. You boyish little backslapper!

SOLDIER: You nail-filer, you hair-comber, you top-of-the-class, hand-in-the-air teacher-pleaser!

GIRL: You one-of-the-lads guffawer, you High Street-staggerer, you gay-baiting, snatch-obsessed boot-polisher!

SOLDIER: Ballet dancer!

GIRL: Pie-chewer!

SOLDIER: Quiche-nibbler!

GIRL: Pitbull-owner!

SOLDIER: Piano-player!

GIRL: Skateboarder!

SOLDIER: (*A sudden plea, a child.*) I'm so lonely, save me!

A huge explosion nearby.

The MOTHER and FATHER cower.

Your beauty and oh, my squalor. Your innocence and oh, my disease. I could be saved by you, yes, I could find peace. Please…let me rinse myself inside you, let me rinse myself in the purity of your soul.

GIRL: Die alone.

SOLDIER: No.

GIRL: In a cold bed with unwashed sheets, with dirty rain down the windows.

SOLDIER: I'm so scared.

GIRL: In the filth of your own ignorance, in the stink of your own stupidity.

SOLDIER: (*Approaching.*) In you I see my future. I see my future, my future, my…

Suddenly a shot is fired from the GIRL's gun. The shattering of glass.

The SOLDIER slowly brings his hand to his ear. There is blood.

GIRL: It was an accident.

SOLDIER: You have, it appears, removed one of my ears.

GIRL: Then I…apologise.

FATHER: That is the first time she has ever apologised.

MOTHER: For anything.

GIRL: It went off by itself.

FATHER: It was an antique mirror.

MOTHER: Nineteenth-century.

FATHER: Been in the family for generations.

MOTHER: But at least we have the other one.

GIRL: Let me bandage it for you.

SOLDIER: No.

GIRL: It's the least I can do.

SOLDIER: I shall not fall for you, gentle enemy.

MOTHER: This is a new side of her.

FATHER: Completely new, yes.

MOTHER: The way she looks at him.

FATHER: The way he looks at her.

MOTHER: They seem unable to tear their gazes from each other.

FATHER: Though the gaze is hostile.

MOTHER: And the words poisonous.

FATHER: Her voice does soften on occasions.

MOTHER: As it has rarely done before.

FATHER: The mysteries of physical attraction perhaps?

MOTHER: Oh, the mysteries.

Suddenly a shot is fired from the SOLDIER's gun.

The GIRL's revolver immediately flies out of her hand and into the wings. The shattering of glass.

MOTHER: The other one.

FATHER: It was an antique mirror.

MOTHER: Nineteenth-century.

FATHER: Been in the family for generations.

MOTHER: Our precious items.

FATHER: Disappearing one by one.

MOTHER: Into oblivion.

FATHER: Possessions are important.

MOTHER: They anchor one down.

FATHER: To one's own life.

MOTHER: Stop one drifting away.

FATHER: And descending into a nomadic barbarism.

MOTHER: Like savages in a cave.

FATHER: Like beasts in the field.

GIRL: You are clearly a good shot.

SOLDIER: Now…raise your glasses.

The FATHER and MOTHER raise their glasses.

The FATHER hands the GIRL a glass.

The SOLDIER covers all three with his rifle.

Raise your glasses, please.

The MOTHER and FATHER slowly raise their glasses.

The GIRL raises her glass.

To freedom, say it!

FATHER: To freedom.

MOTHER: To freedom.

SOLDIER: And you. Say it.

The GIRL slowly raises her glass to her mouth. She remains silent. With his gun trained at her head, she looks at him with contempt.

(*Screaming.*) To freedom!!

She seems on the verge of saying something. Then she drops the glass. It shatters.

Blackout. In the darkness the sound of helicopters overhead and distant explosions.

Part Three

Some time later. The ruins of the house. The GIRL, in despair, holds a knife to her belly. The MOTHER stands close by. She makes the sign of the cross. The family are now wearing dirty, tattered clothing. Isolated gunfire throughout. The occasional helicopter, searchlight. The screams of the wounded and dying throughout.

GIRL: And that is why this thing, this throbbing maggot in my guts... that is why it must now...

MOTHER: Spare me the details...

GIRL: Oh, how he lurched at me. How he staggered.

MOTHER: Not again, I implore you!

GIRL: Then his tongue in my ear, his blood-caked palm on my mouth.

MOTHER: (*Hands over ears.*) Every day, every day...

GIRL: His panting, like a dog, like some slavering hound.

MOTHER: We really must try to discuss other topics.

GIRL: His hand over my mouth, smothering my screaming, his hand on my legs, on my back, round my waist. Dirtying my delicate flesh. And then this tongue, this living slug of meat thrust deep down my throat.

MOTHER: We must tell your father!

GIRL: And then I'm on my back and he's on me, he's in me. He is in me, Mother! We thrash. We clash. He's tugging my hair, my lips bleeding. My head gripped as if in a vice. And him like a hog, like a grunting hog in some stinking sty, pounding and bellowing, nostrils flaring, enjoying my terror, intoxicated by the stench of my pain. Our hips colliding, our ribs scraping.

MOTHER: (*Approaching.*) We thought you were safe.

GIRL: Don't touch.

MOTHER: That you were showing him your books.

GIRL: A tour of my library!?

MOTHER: Yes!

GIRL: At gunpoint!?

MOTHER: Your prized editions.

GIRL: With a gun at my head!

MOTHER: I must hold you.

GIRL: And he touched me, Mother…

MOTHER: I must, how I must!

GIRL: As we mounted the stairs.

MOTHER: Let me love you.

GIRL: The muzzle of his gun in the small of my back.

MOTHER: I am here for you.

GIRL: Don't touch.

MOTHER: I must embrace you. I must, please God, have some
    minor function!

GIRL: One step closer and this blade will be shaving the soft
    and unformed skull of your little relative here, cutting into
    its tender tissues…

MOTHER: Despite everything the child is still the Divine…

GIRL: It sucks the life from me.

MOTHER: Is still the Divine once again longing for itself.

GIRL: Drains me.

MOTHER: Love me, I implore you.

GIRL: Weakens me.

MOTHER: I simply have to hold you in my arms.

GIRL: Back!

MOTHER: Let me shoulder just a portion of your pain.

GIRL: You merely comfort yourself in the cloying embrace.

MOTHER: Grant me just a little touch of your agony.

GIRL: You would simply burden me with your own anxieties.

MOTHER: I need my routines back.

GIRL: And I have so little strength.

MOTHER: My cooking, my canasta.

GIRL: And all I possess this monster bleeds from me.

MOTHER: Now we are starving.

GIRL: This evil!

MOTHER: Hear this then! Last night…last night, your father struck me. It was the first time. But it was my fault. I tend to annoy. You know that. Yes, I was weeping and I found it hard to stop. This situation. The way our lives have turned out. I have craved…intimacy. Thought it was my right. But it came to me last night. I shall never know it. Perhaps it's a myth. I hope it is a myth since I should not like to be missing out on something to which others have such easy access. It all became too much and the tears welled up. He was trying to sleep. He asked me to stop. The sniffles, the sobs, the gulping down of all this unhappiness, this disappointment, the dull ache of which deepens every day. But I could not. Stop. I ached for comfort. His scrawny pajamed arm over my chest even, his digital watch cold against my chin, to feel just his bony knee brushing against my thigh even. Small things. A knuckle on my stomach even, lips just lightly on the back of my neck even, steady life-affirming exhalations in my ear but…no, nothing. And so I wept. Sounds of the shooting and the helicopters and the screams of the wounded all around. The intrusive beams of the searchlights. But it was my stifled crying that disturbed him more. And then after a while he simply exploded.

GIRL: This is your confession, Mother!?

MOTHER: He never wanted to resemble his father. Hates the fact that they share the same haunted look, the same asymmetrical features. Even to the way he adjusts his crotch or hawks at his nose. His father to a tee. And these traits he has worked so assiduously to eradicate. But now…they really are like peas in a pod. But you have to know the truth. Say nothing to him. He is a good man really. He has supported us well and over these long years he has made numerous astute financial investments.

GIRL: Your little, little confession…

MOTHER: And now I have turned once again to the Creator. As a child I would draw happy little scenes from the Bible. With my set of coloured crayons. (*Pause.*) I just thought you should know.

A silence. The GIRL makes ready to stab herself in the guts.

The MOTHER looks on helplessly. The GIRL brings the knife back, ready to strike. She closes her eyes. A searchlight sweeps across the stage.

Oh, why can I never ever…do? Why? Why?

The FATHER enters, triumphantly holding a dead cat by the tail.

FATHER: It is the man's responsibility, is it not, to bring home the bacon?

MOTHER: Is that not next-door's cat!?

FATHER: The thing was sluggish, emaciated, sitting on a crumbling wall. I staggered past. It arched its back up towards me expecting some affection. Without thinking I gathered it up in my arms, hurried it into what's left of my garden shed and crushed its skull with a power tool.

MOTHER: What have you done?

FATHER: Then I saw the girls next door, through a gap in the fence, come looking for their pet. Calling its name. Weeping with worry. I felt nothing.

MOTHER: What have we become?

FATHER: Skin it.

MOTHER: I cannot eat this cat.

FATHER: We have not eaten for days.

MOTHER: I have known it since kittenhood.

FATHER: Skin it, gut it.

MOTHER: I remember the faces of those girls when it first frolicked from its box.

FATHER: (*To the GIRL.*) Then pass me that knife.

GIRL: This knife has a more important mission.

MOTHER: Your daughter has a revelation.

FATHER: Yes?

MOTHER: She is…

Massive explosions, shouting, screaming etc…

…with child.

A long silence.

FATHER: She is…?

MOTHER: With child. Yes.

Massive explosions, shouting, screaming etc…

FATHER: I cannot…understand… We raised her to be…

Massive explosions, shouting, screaming etc…

We have to keep control of ourselves. As a family. Keep strong. And now you say…

MOTHER: And there is more.

FATHER: The honour of the family. She is only a child. And now this, she is like a whore in a war zone, some bitch in the night, offering up her body.

GIRL: Wife-beater! Woman-hater! Coward, weakling, bully!

MOTHER (*To the GIRL.*) / FATHER (*To the MOTHER.*): What are you saying?

GIRL: You hit my mother!

MOTHER (*To the GIRL.*) / FATHER (*To the MOTHER.*): What are you saying?

GIRL: The enemy you will not fight.

FATHER: I am too weak to fight.

GIRL: But your own wife you can happily hit!

FATHER: What are you telling her?

MOTHER: (*Changing subject.*) I shall now disembowel this creature. Roast it with some mint.

FATHER: I am a keen admirer of mint. I rank it very highly indeed.

MOTHER: Though not as highly as dill?

FATHER: Not as highly as dill, no.

MOTHER: Dill is certainly your favourite.

FATHER: But herbs must always be fresh.

MOTHER: Of course they must.

FATHER: I simply cannot countenance dried herbs from those tiny supermarket jars.

MOTHER: Then pass it to me.

The FATHER holds out the cat to her.

The MOTHER thinks about taking it. She cannot.

A massive explosion.

FATHER: Take the cat.

MOTHER: I cannot.

FATHER: Take the cat.

MOTHER: No.

FATHER: And will you give me that knife?

GIRL: I cannot.

FATHER: Give me the knife.

GIRL: No.

FATHER: So I see now I have no influence whatsoever over my family?

GIRL: Quiet! I want you both to see.

A long silence as she makes ready to stab herself again.

FATHER: What in God's name are you doing?

She brings back the knife.

(*To MOTHER.*) Does she mean to kill herself?

Eventually, her will dissolving, she drops the knife.

Then I…

He picks up the knife and makes ready to skin the cat. An explosion nearby.

MOTHER: Why can we not just surrender? Do we not know we are beaten?

GIRL: (*Very weak.*) There will be no surrender.

FATHER: I assume your absurd vegetarianism bars you from joining us for supper tonight?

GIRL: It was a pleasant, friendly cat.

MOTHER: It gave those girls so much pleasure.

FATHER: But we simply must eat.

He takes the knife and again prepares to make an incision. A silence.

MOTHER: Then do it!

FATHER: Quiet!

GIRL: Just do it then!

FATHER: Quiet, I say!

With an extreme effort of will, he makes a final attempt. Eventually defeated, he gives up and drops the knife.

FATHER: We must persevere with potatoes.

MOTHER: But the ground is so hard. We cannot dig them up.

FATHER: And the rubble and dust have ruined the herb garden.

MOTHER: But mint like the cockroaches will always survive.

FATHER: We need a miracle.

MOTHER: But you don't believe in such things…

FATHER: We need a miracle now!!!

He sinks to his knees in despair. The MOTHER makes the sign of the cross. She sinks to her knees in prayer.

MOTHER: Dear Lord…

As she continues her prayer:

FATHER: What in God's name is she doing?

GIRL: She is praying for a miracle. She has rediscovered her faith.

FATHER: This is madness. This is, and always has been, a secular family.

GIRL: It comforts her.

FATHER: It is illusion, delusion.

GIRL: For cowards and imbeciles.

FATHER: It affronts me to see people on their knees.

He realises he too is on his knees and stands.

Who is he then? This man who has ruined you.

No response.

And so I assume then that you…love him?

The GIRL lets out a surprised laugh. The laugh builds. It echoes across the stage. The MOTHER continues to pray. Explosions continue. The FATHER is still holding the cat by the tail.

Stop it, the pair of you! Desist this instant! You, stop your praying! It is insane, medieval! And you, stop your laughing. I am your father, your husband. I am all you revere. I have made such sacrifices and you laugh. And you pray! I have suffered for you and you laugh. And you pray! A lifetime in an office and you laugh! For you! And for you! And you laugh! And you pray! This dull stability, which I have created from the sweat of my brow, has been all for you! And you laugh, and you pray!

The GIRL's laughter eventually peters out.

Now ask your mother to stop this pathetic display.

MOTHER: …please grant us mercy in this, the hour of our greatest need.

FATHER: Will you get off your knees, fool?!

MOTHER: (*Rising, moved.*) Any moment now I feel we shall be delivered.

FATHER: There is no such thing as a miracle.

Now the SOLDIER appears in a blaze of light. Religious music. He is no longer a wild man in military gear but wears a boilersuit and holds a spanner. A factory worker. His manner has changed and so has his accent.

SOLDIER: Since, sir, you no longer have a door I did not, indeed I could not, knock.

GIRL: Get out of this house!

SOLDIER: I trust you do not mind my intrusion, sir, madam?

GIRL: Get out of this house!

FATHER: What can we do for you?

SOLDIER: You do not remember me?

FATHER: No.

SOLDIER: My appearance was a little different on our last meeting.

GIRL: Get out!

FATHER: Please forgive our daughter. She is delirious with hunger.

GIRL: Get him out!

SOLDIER: I have changed my career.

FATHER: I see.

SOLDIER: And with it my demeanour.

MOTHER: Rapist! Murderer!

The MOTHER hurls herself at the SOLDIER and tries to punch him wildly. The SOLDIER fends her off, gently, expertly.

You have destroyed my daughter!

FATHER: What in God's name are you doing?!

MOTHER: You savage, you filthy savage!

SOLDIER: I am here to assist, madam.

MOTHER: Lout! Savage! Animal!

The FATHER grabs his wife and tries to pull her off the SOLDIER. Man and wife fall to the floor and wrestle furiously for a time. The wrestling becomes a violent fight and is soon spiralling out of control. Over this:

SOLDIER: I am in love.

GIRL: You are not welcome here!

SOLDIER: I am in love with you.

GIRL: You are not welcome here!

SOLDIER: I have tried to fight it.

GIRL: You are not welcome here!

SOLDIER: But I am unable to.

GIRL: You are not welcome here!

SOLDIER: I dream of you.

GIRL: You are not welcome here!

SOLDIER: Because of you I have given up the life. I tired of all the torture. I am now engaged in honest labour. But I do have ambition. I know a girl likes a man with ambition. They are preparing things for when the war is over. For when the regime has been restored.

GIRL: You are not welcome here!

SOLDIER: The economy will swagger again.

GIRL: You are not welcome here!

SOLDIER: I want to provide you all with a life. When this is finished. I can protect you.

GIRL: You are not welcome here!

SOLDIER: I lie there at night in my painful solitude, in the restless dark, and it is you that I see, it is you that I taste, it is you that I smell. And that beautiful voice.

GIRL: You raped me!

SOLDIER: I am so in love with you.

GIRL: You raped me! You raped me! You raped me!!

She breaks for a time and then:

(*Screaming at her parents.*) Dear God, will you please stop fighting!?

The SOLDIER pulls the flailing MOTHER off the FATHER. He then helps the man to his feet.

The couple stand opposite each other, panting.

SOLDIER: Why don't you put down the cat, sir?

FATHER: Yes.

The FATHER continues to hold it by the tail.

SOLDIER: You do not need to eat your pets.

FATHER: It is not ours.

MOTHER: It belongs to our neighbours.

SOLDIER: I saw you earlier, sir.

FATHER: Did you?

SOLDIER: Scraping it up off the road.

MOTHER: What?!!

SOLDIER: Furtive looks around. Hoping no one saw you stooping so low.

MOTHER: You told us you killed it!

The GIRL laughs through her tears.

FATHER: Please…do not laugh at me!

GIRL: I felt a spasm of admiration for you, a shudder of respect when I thought that you had…

MOTHER: He told us he killed it.

SOLDIER: It was probably sheltering under a tank and perhaps, spying a potential mate, it bounded from its sanctuary, in search of relief, just as the machine rolled forth and the treads…

MOTHER: Why did you tell us you killed it?

SOLDIER: You don't need to eat cat just yet, sir. Here…I have something for you.

GIRL: You are not welcome here!

SOLDIER: Without my help you will starve.

GIRL: You are not welcome here!

SOLDIER: I cannot let this happen to such good people.

MOTHER: He violated my daughter!

SOLDIER: Here.

He opens his briefcase and takes out a string of sausages.

I have here some sausages, sir. I can get you a chicken tomorrow. Then next week I am hopeful of securing other, more luxurious provisions.

MOTHER: Perhaps a little pâté?

GIRL: You are not welcome here!

SOLDIER: My love…

GIRL: You are not welcome here!

SOLDIER: I feel so happy.

FATHER: Will you please wait a moment?

MOTHER: Do you not understand what he has done to her? To your own daughter!

The GIRL runs off, distraught.

SOLDIER: You must see what is happening outside? Corpses in the street, sir, snow falling onto the blue, bloated bodies. Children, sir, skin and bone, crawling along the kerbs in search of scraps. Dying pathetically there with swollen bellies and bulging eyeballs. The bodies are piling up, sir. It's a field day for the crows and the ravens and the rats. They won't lift this blockade until the coup is overthrown, the counter-revolution complete.

FATHER: Oh God…

SOLDIER: You have no health service, sir, no transport. The insurgents, indeed your very own neighbours, they have somehow polluted the water supply. Your farmers went out of business years ago. You can't live on just what you grow in your gardens. The island is surrounded, nothing can get through.

MOTHER: We will manage.

SOLDIER: The Free World means you no harm but they just preferred things as they were. Do not waste your lives fighting the inevitable. Embrace the system, enjoy its advantages and then count your blessings. Better surely to fill your bellies in an imperfect world.

MOTHER: But you…my daughter…you…!

SOLDIER: And live.

MOTHER: But you…

SOLDIER: I came here to offer you my assistance.

FATHER: Why would you help us?

SOLDIER: I require responsibilities, I require someone to look after me, someone to look after. I require a family. Each night, when I am through with the world of work, I require a soft bosom and a sweet smile to come home to. I do not wish to sit alone in front of the television with one hand down my trousers and the other surfing channels, nor do I wish to drink myself to death with other lonely men. No, sir. I require a listening ear for my anxieties. And I am offering you my support. I am now in a position to make your lives more... (*A long pause as he chooses.*) ...comfortable.

FATHER/MOTHER: We so love comfort!

SOLDIER: I have fallen in love.

FATHER: You are young.

SOLDIER: I know what is right.

MOTHER: But time will alter you.

SOLDIER: For me and for her.

FATHER: Your life is before you.

SOLDIER: I know about life. I know about love.

MOTHER: But time will alter you.

FATHER: The person you say you love will soon become...

MOTHER: A dead weight around your days.

FATHER: Marriage is a terrible burden.

MOTHER: A delusion of youth.

FATHER: A trap laid by our genes.

MOTHER: A horrible trick.

FATHER: The drug wears off.

MOTHER: So quickly.

FATHER: You think you've free will.

MOTHER: But you're just a machine!

FATHER: A machine for your genes!

MOTHER: And now one always feels one is missing out.

FATHER: There is a lack.

MOTHER: A hole in one's life.

FATHER: Thoughts are always of what might have been.

MOTHER: Had one not in one's idealistic days so rashly diminished one's options.

FATHER: Oh, the regret!

MOTHER: The regret...

FATHER: ...the regret!

MOTHER: We lacked direction.

FATHER: Were at a loss.

MOTHER: I was so lonely.

FATHER: So at a loss.

MOTHER: So alone.

FATHER: Life is elsewhere.

MOTHER: Oh, it is...elsewhere!

FATHER: I needed an audience.

MOTHER: And I needed a child.

FATHER: Someone to mother me and make me hot soup.

BOTH: What else was there for us to do?

FATHER: We lacked imagination.

MOTHER: And the stomach for an existence alone.

FATHER: Now I dream always of other women.

MOTHER: And I other men.

FATHER: Much younger flesh.

MOTHER: A kind man to hold me.

FATHER: As a youth I simply did not have sufficient sexual intercourse.

MOTHER: A little touch of kindness in the night.

FATHER: This is my greatest regret.

MOTHER: I have only known your father.

SOLDIER: But he is not my father.

FATHER: My greatest regret.

MOTHER: My greatest regret.

FATHER: Yes, my greatest regret.

MOTHER: It's my greatest regret.

SOLDIER: You shall not dissuade me.

FATHER: Everyone thinks they can win.

MOTHER: But nobody does.

FATHER: Only the bastards think they are winning.

SOLDIER: I can offer you a job.

FATHER: A job?

SOLDIER: But there are dangers. Collaborators, as the terrorists will term you, are being mercilessly targeted.

MOTHER: The terrorists?

SOLDIER: The teachers, the binmen…

FATHER: A time-killing, day-filling job?

SOLDIER: The students and street-sweepers…

FATHER: Oh, the joy! Oh, the sweet tedium!

SOLDIER: Librarians, poets.

FATHER: It will pattern my weeks!

SOLDIER: You will input data.

FATHER: I adore data entry.

SOLDIER: Itemise weapons.

FATHER: I adore data entry.

SOLDIER: Parts for the tanks, for the warheads, the guns.

FATHER: I adore data entry.

SOLDIER: We're exporting munitions.

FATHER: I adore data entry.

SOLDIER: To the Arabs and blacks.

FATHER: I adore data entry.

SOLDIER: Governments must all now learn to protect
themselves from the wills of their people.

MOTHER: You cannot accept this man's help!

FATHER: But we must live.

MOTHER: Tell me you are innocent.

SOLDIER: I am a good Christian man.

MOTHER: A good Christian man?

SOLDIER: A good Christian man.

Massive explosions, aircraft etc.

MOTHER: A good Christian man, you say?

SOLDIER: A good Christian man.

MOTHER: A good Christian man?

Massive explosions, aircraft etc.

SOLDIER: A good Christian man.

MOTHER: A good Christian man?

FATHER: I adore data entry.

SOLDIER: A good Christian man.

They do not speak.

Massive explosions, aircraft etc.

MOTHER: A good Christian man, you say?

SOLDIER: A good Christian man.

FATHER: I adore data entry.

SOLDIER: Then come to the ruins of the hospital tomorrow. Eight a.m. You'll be escorted under armed guard to the warehouse.

MOTHER: What is the wage?

SOLDIER: It is drudgery, sir but it is steady.

FATHER: I adore data entry.

MOTHER: A good, Christian man?

FATHER: And do forgive our daughter's rudeness!

SOLDIER: I am in love with her.

FATHER: Your kindness shall not be forgotten.

SOLDIER: So why don't you give me the cat, sir?

FATHER: I adore data entry.

The SOLDIER takes the cat. He puts the bag down.

SOLDIER: Your lives are now secure.

FATHER: I adore data entry.

SOLDIER: You said.

FATHER: It is something for which I know I have an affinity.

SOLDIER: I shall see you tomorrow then…Father.

FATHER: I adore data entry.

SOLDIER: For the start of your new career.

FATHER: And we can swap the sad, sad stories of our formative years?

SOLDIER: Of course.

FATHER: Over a pint? In the snug? With a log fire blazing away?

SOLDIER: Of course.

FATHER: And the words tumbling out of our mouths, loosened by the dark, golden ale, our friendship cemented with every trip to the bar?

SOLDIER: Of course.

FATHER: I adore data entry.

SOLDIER: And I shall return soon.

FATHER: I adore data entry.

SOLDIER: To conquer the heart of your beautiful daughter.

He leaves, taking the cat with him.

A long silence.

FATHER: I adore data entry.

MOTHER: You said.

FATHER: It is something for which I know I have an affinity.

MOTHER: A good Christian man.

FATHER: It is something for which I know I have an affinity.

MOTHER: A good Christian man, he said?

FATHER: I adore data entry.

MOTHER: You said.

FATHER: It is something for which I know I have an affinity.

MOTHER: What's in the bag?

FATHER: Sausages, he said. Such kindness.

MOTHER: But our daughter maintains...?

FATHER: I adore data entry.

MOTHER: No, a good Christian man...

FATHER: It is something for which I know I have an affinity.

She approaches the bag. Slowly she puts her arm inside. He signals to her that he is to do the inspection, again a Hardy to her Laurel. He goes to the bag. He pulls out a string of sausages. They stare at each other. Then the MOTHER makes a lunge for the sausages. Takes them from him and brings them to her mouth, eating frantically. He grabs the string, tugs it from her and eats. She does it again. Then he does it. They end up performing a strange tug-of-war, all the time devouring the raw sausages like animals. Soon they are on the floor, struggling for control of the food.

Blackout.

A little machine-gun fire in the darkness.

Part Four

Months later. The odd helicopter but no gunfire, no explosions. The GIRL, now heavily pregnant, is sat up in bed. She screams in agony. She is very weak, starving, delirious.

GIRL: I shall certainly resist this. Though thoughts are always of food. But I shall not sup with the devil. Would rather die than drink from his table. Oh, stop all this stamping, these random acts of violence! Why are you so vicious? I have given you everything and all you do is cause me pain. But soon I shall force you out slithering and savage into this sewer of a world and you shall suffer and you shall hurt. We are at odds, are we not, since I with all my soul wish to depart this life, while you are endeavouring with such a violent impatience to gain an invitation? And in time you may even become a trader! Yes, some high-fiving trader with your winking and greedy eye upon the world, upon the material world. But no, I shall not be here to enquire as to your health or to make sure you wear warm enough clothes in the winter.

She screams in agony.

Enter the MOTHER triumphantly in an extravagant hat and dress, high heels and handbag.

MOTHER: Today is to be a day of celebration! Will you not eat?

GIRL: Only what I get from the ground.

MOTHER: But your crops are still failing. Will you not eat?

GIRL: Let me die with them.

MOTHER: Your father and I dined with the head of the department. We had cured salmon with a crayfish mousse. Will you not eat?

GIRL: You look ridiculous.

MOTHER: It seems he has already so impressed his superiors that some form of promotion is soon to be upon us. Will you not eat? And the father of the child has now been informed. What do you think of these gloves?

GIRL: No!!

MOTHER: I could not contain my excitement. When one reaches a certain age one becomes a little obsessed with becoming a grandparent.

GIRL: I was raped!

MOTHER: He's nice and polite and in love and so nice and he's such a hard worker, so nice and hardworking, this man is so nice and his nice and bright office, the thirty-third floor and its nice panorama, the lovely blue sea, and those white-painted walls, and its nice water cooler, the yucca plants yes and the nice herbal tea.

GIRL: He raped me!

MOTHER: Every week he comes to call, and oh he has such a nice voice now, the smooth velvet voice of a judge or a fox-hunter, and every week you refuse even to acknowledge him. Will you not eat?

GIRL: Please God…

MOTHER: This man is so nice, he has saved us, so nice. Would you rather be dead?

GIRL: I long for my death…

MOTHER: This man is so nice and he wept, he's so nice, how we wept, how we wept on his blueberry pie, I was seated close by so I eased his sweet pain, with a rub of the back and a nice caring smile, he winked at me yes through his eyes filled with tears and he squeezed my pale hand and I felt such a love.

GIRL: You populate the occupied land and you spawn fat generations, oblivious as you stuff your faces, oblivious to the bones and the blood beneath your feet and the murdered flesh that will make your grass grow.

MOTHER: We played bridge and drank a little brandy.

GIRL: Grass to feed the cows to make your meat.

MOTHER: My sweet, sweet routine…

GIRL: The living will consume the dead…

MOTHER: Tomorrow we have a dream kitchen fitted. A Formica top with a marble effect. The chandeliers are to be repaired and the wall outside rebuilt. A gang of men are to spend the day removing the multi-coloured cluster bombs embedded in that crescent of earth by the patio. Will you not eat?

GIRL: I shall…

MOTHER: While I am being brought a whole host of seeds to revitalise the garden.

GIRL: …resist.

MOTHER: Nasturtiums and sunflowers, sweet peas and marigolds.

GIRL: I shall always…

MOTHER: Hollyhocks, pansies, lupins and lavender.

GIRL: …say No.

MOTHER: Your father has friends now, your father has friends and he's not so concerned for the state of the world and he's taking up golf and he's taking up golf and will you not eat, tell me will you not eat, I feel much less alone now, yes, much less alone and he's taking up golf and he's taking up golf and will you not eat, tell me will you not eat and he's not so concerned for the state of the world…

FATHER: (*Entering in golf gear with a newspaper open.*) Since what can you do, tell me, what can you do?

MOTHER: Since what can you do?

FATHER: I am taking up golf.

MOTHER: He is taking up golf.

FATHER: I'm now not so concerned for the state of the world...

MOTHER: ...and he's taking up golf.

FATHER: I am taking up golf.

MOTHER: Since what can you do?

FATHER: Tell me, what can you do?

MOTHER: For the state of the world?

FATHER: For the state of the world.

MOTHER: He's now not so concerned.

FATHER: I am taking up golf.

The GIRL screams in agony. Silence.

MOTHER: Speak then. Won't you speak? Please. Tell us. What is happening. In the world.

FATHER: It is quite extraordinary.

MOTHER: It is?

FATHER: The war is over.

MOTHER: Then let us celebrate.

She goes to him. They stand close together.

The sound of an army marching past. After a time:

A kiss then?

FATHER: A kiss?

MOTHER: A kiss. Yes.

FATHER: (*After a pause.*) I think not.

MOTHER: No?

FATHER: No.

MOTHER: No kiss?

FATHER: Not today.

MOTHER: Might I ask why not?

FATHER: (*After a pause.*) I am tired.

MOTHER: Then how was your day?

FATHER: Tedious but comforting. Secure in the knowledge of the regular wage.

MOTHER: Because the money goes in.

FATHER: Yes, the money goes in.

MOTHER: On the twenty-sixth of each month.

FATHER: The fifteenth.

MOTHER: I thought the twenty-sixth?

FATHER: No. The fifteenth.

MOTHER: (*After a pause.*) It used to be the twenty-sixth.

FATHER: But now it is the fifteenth.

MOTHER: I am so proud of you.

FATHER: The salary is quite…extraordinary.

MOTHER: Such a relief.

FATHER: I feel finally part of a family.

MOTHER: Your colleagues are so…nice.

FATHER: I have never been so happy.

MOTHER: So…let us celebrate.

She goes to him. They stand close together. The sound of an army marching past. After a time:

A kiss then?

FATHER: A kiss?

MOTHER: A kiss. Yes.

FATHER: (*After a pause.*) I think not.

MOTHER: No?

FATHER: No.

MOTHER: No kiss?

FATHER: Not today.

MOTHER: Might I ask why not?

FATHER: (*After a pause.*) I am tired.

The sound of an army marching past.

Quite extraordinary.

MOTHER: It is?

FATHER: The Prime Minister has been reinstalled after almost a year incarcerated. He says he has learned from the experience, grown in both spirit and faith like that South African black. He says he can forgive his enemies. He has urged mercy be shown to those who illegally deposed him.

MOTHER: A good, Christian man.

FATHER: He is looking forward to seeing his family again.

MOTHER: His nice family, his nice and smiling and optimistic family…

FATHER: He thanks the Free World for once again coming to the aid of liberal democracy in its hour of need and regrets the fanaticism, this demented delusion of socialism, which has brought so much destruction to the people of his beloved country.

The GIRL screams in agony.

I am taking up golf.

MOTHER: You are taking up golf.

FATHER: I'm now not so concerned for the state of the world…

MOTHER: …and you're taking up golf.

FATHER: I am taking up golf.

MOTHER: Since what can you do?

FATHER: Yes, what can you do?

The GIRL screams in agony.

MOTHER: We are doing well. Yes? You and I? Doing well. In our lives? Doing well? Look at what we have. Compared to the others. We are doing well? You and I? Compared to the others. We have lived our lives wisely? We have lived our lives well? I should say yes. All things considered? Yes? Doing quite well. Compared to the others. You and I? Our marriage is strong. Would you not say?

The SOLDIER now bursts onto the stage. He is now in a smart suit. He carries a bottle of champagne and a large bouquet of flowers. He now has the smooth velvet voice of a judge or a fox-hunter.

SOLDIER: I simply have to see my beloved. You simply have to let me see her.

GIRL: Get out of my country!!!

SOLDIER: Pray…why did you not tell me sooner?

GIRL: Get out of my country!!!

SOLDIER: My life is now centred here upon this very bed. You are everything I am living for. My future, my dreams!

GIRL: Get out of my country!!!

SOLDIER: And now this child, this fruit of my loins, this fruit of our love.

GIRL: Get out of my country!!!

The GIRL screams in agony again.

The MOTHER now begins to twist round, inspecting her dress and hat as if in a mirror. She readjusts her hat, readjusts her dress, takes her gloves on and off, all the time twisting, checking her figure. The FATHER, on the other side, practises his swing. They move in time together, a grotesque comic dance. In the centre the bed.

SOLDIER: I am invited to meetings. On long, polished tables of varnished wood, of oak. Pristine white pads of paper set at every place as if in the finest of restaurants, company biros, bottles of mineral water direct from the Alps. A nervous Filipino woman serves us coffee, serves us Colombian filter coffee and shortbread biscuits. And we discuss. We deliberate. We debate. Strategy, targets, market fluctuations. Flip charts, flow charts, graphs and projections. I am involved. I contribute.

GIRL: Get out of my country!!!

SOLDIER: We will have such a life, you and I.

GIRL: Get out of my country!!!

SOLDIER: Holidays abroad, cruises to the Pacific.

GIRL: Get out of my country!!!

SOLDIER: Visits to the great capitals. The great European capitals.

GIRL: Get out of my country!!!

SOLDIER: Paris. Prague. Vienna. Rome. Steep ourselves in the history of it all. Theatre, opera, ballet, books.

GIRL: Get out of my country!!!

SOLDIER: We are young and we are beautiful.

She screams in agony.

We will trek the jungles and we shall shoot the rapids and we shall dive the many oceans.

GIRL: Get out of my country!!!

SOLDIER: Just tell me to go and I shall go.

GIRL: Get out of my country!!!

SOLDIER: Just tell me to go and I shall go.

GIRL: Get out of my country!!!

SOLDIER: All has worked out for the best.

GIRL: Get out of my country!!!

SOLDIER: In time you shall see.

GIRL: Get out of my country!!!

SOLDIER: That night, it was for me a defining moment. All pretence stripped away. Just us alone, alone in our immaculate desire.

GIRL: You raped me!!

SOLDIER: You cannot deny your feelings.

SOLDIER/FATHER/MOTHER: She doesn't know what's best for her.

MOTHER: What's in her own interests.

FATHER: There's nothing wrong with comfort.

MOTHER: Nothing wrong with consolation…

SOLDIER: I so love you, my darling.

The GIRL spits in his face.

(*Smiling, oblivious.*) I love you to the ends of the earth.

The GIRL spits in his face.

Take a look at this suit, the cut of the cloth. My watch is gold-plated, the haircut one I procured from that new salon that's sprung from the ruins of the old church. My shoes were not cheap.

GIRL: Get out of my country!!!

MOTHER: Oh, he has the smooth velvet voice of a judge or a fox-hunter.

GIRL: Get out of my country!!!

SOLDIER: I shall support you in the full and true flowering of your own potential. I shall be the rain that nourishes the earth of you, the sea that laps against the sand of you. You can be anything you want to be.

GIRL: Get out of my country!!!

SOLDIER: But we must now build the peace. A world united under one ideal. The ideal of free trade.

GIRL: Get out of my country!!!

SOLDIER: And the heaping-up of capital.

GIRL: (*A scream that is amplified and echoed across the stage.*) No! No! Please God, no! There must be more to this life than that!! There is surely more to this life than that!!!

When the last echo fades:

The SOLDIER laughs. It is echoed and amplified and resonates around the stage. The laughter soon becomes the mocking laughter of an ever-growing crowd.

The GIRL screams in agony.

The sound of an army marching past. The laughter continues through the following dialogue.

The MOTHER and FATHER still engaged, she in twisting in the mirror, and he in practising his golf swing.

GIRL: Why do you laugh? Why do you laugh?

The GIRL screams in agony.

The sound of an army marching past.

FATHER: Will she never grow up?

MOTHER: So childish, naïve!

FATHER: Will she never grow up? I am taking up golf.

MOTHER: Does it flatter my hips?

FATHER: I'm now not so concerned for the state of the world.

MOTHER: Does it flatter my bust?

FATHER: I am taking up golf.

MOTHER: The pearls or the chain?

FATHER: I am taking up golf.

MOTHER: You are taking up golf.

FATHER: Since what can you do, tell me…

MOTHER: And I need some new shoes.

FATHER: Tell me, what can you do?

The GIRL screams in agony.

The sound of an army marching past.

GIRL: Why do you laugh? Why do you laugh?

The sound of an army marching past.

The laughter builds.

MOTHER: I am joining a book club.

FATHER: I'm now not so concerned for the state of the world.

MOTHER: And pottery classes.

FATHER: I am taking up golf.

MOTHER: French conversation.

FATHER: Since what can you do?

MOTHER: The world is our oyster.

FATHER: And it's time to start living.

MOTHER: Yes, it's time to begin.

>*The GIRL screams in agony.*
>
>*The sound of an army marching past.*
>
>*The laughter builds.*

GIRL: Why do you laugh?

>*The GIRL screams in agony.*
>
>*The sound of an army marching past.*

MOTHER: The Twinning Committee!

FATHER: Since what can you do?

MOTHER: The Clever Dogs Club!

FATHER: I am taking up golf.

MOTHER: The Fuchsia Society!

FATHER: I am taking up golf.

>*The GIRL screams in agony.*
>
>*The sound of an army marching past.*

GIRL: Why do you laugh? Why do you laugh? (*Screaming.*)
WHY WHY WHY DO YOU LAUGH?

The laughter of the crowd ends. The MOTHER stops twisting in the mirror, the FATHER his golf swing.

SOLDIER: We must now make this official.

The sound of an army marching past.

The SOLDIER goes to the bed. He places the flowers on the bed. The bed and the GIRL disappear into darkness.

The SOLDIER, still holding the champagne, begins to march from one side of the stage to the other.

The MOTHER goes to the FATHER. They stand close together.

MOTHER: A kiss then?

FATHER: A kiss?

MOTHER: A kiss. Yes.

FATHER: (*After a pause.*) I think not.

MOTHER: No?

FATHER: No.

MOTHER: No kiss?

FATHER: No kiss. Not today.

MOTHER: Might I ask why not?

The sound of an army marching past.

FATHER: I look upon you and your ageing body, your ever-whitening hair, your numerous ailments…and it is all a constant reminder that my days are almost done.

MOTHER: It is merely…

FATHER: And so consequently…

MOTHER: …a touch of arthritis.

FATHER: And so consequently I am abandoning you.

MOTHER: Merely…

FATHER: It is not the fact of my own middle age that causes me pain. Rather it is the fact of yours. Also…

SOLDIER: I feel like a boy again!

FATHER: I am taking up golf.

SOLDIER: On a Saturday morning!

FATHER: I am taking up golf.

SOLDIER: The day spread out before me!

FATHER: I'm now not so concerned for the state of the world…

SOLDIER: Stretching out forever!

FATHER: Since what can you do, tell me…

SOLDIER: An eternity in a single day!

FATHER: Tell me, what can you do?

SOLDIER: I am recapturing my youth!

FATHER: I resent you growing old.

SOLDIER: No man need remain in the gutter!

FATHER: And I have met someone else.

SOLDIER: Oh, we three, my darling!

FATHER: She is our daughter's age.

SOLDIER: We beautiful three!

FATHER: And oh how she wants me.

SOLDIER: I shall not be like other men.

FATHER: Says she needs me.

SOLDIER: I shall rise above the failings of my sex.

FATHER: The dull stability I represent.

SOLDIER: She will be enough for me.

FATHER: The money on the fifteenth of each month.

SOLDIER: I know about love. I know about life.

FATHER: Oiling the wheels of my modest machine.

SOLDIER: It's in her own interests.

FATHER: She will care for me as I wither and die.

SOLDIER: Soon she will learn.

FATHER: I'm now not so concerned for the state of the world.

SOLDIER: It's in her own interests.

FATHER: She has low self-esteem…

SOLDIER: And what a father I shall be!

FATHER: Has, like you, a tendency to tears.

SOLDIER: A boy moulded after me.

FATHER: To cut at her wrists with a knife, with a nail…

SOLDIER: And all will be well…

FATHER: But her tender flesh, oh how it makes me feel a part of this world.

SOLDIER: The future is bright…

FATHER: I am taking up golf.

SOLDIER: The future is bright…

FATHER: I am taking up golf.

SOLDIER: The future is bright…

FATHER: She works at the club.

SOLDIER: It's in her own interests.

FATHER: I'm now not so concerned for the state of the world.

SOLDIER: Soon she will learn.

FATHER: Since what can you do, tell me…

SOLDIER: Soon she will see.

FATHER: What can you do?

SOLDIER: I know about love. I know about life.

FATHER: I appreciate your support.

SOLDIER: It's in her own interests.

FATHER: These last twenty years.

SOLDIER: The future is bright…

FATHER: Your wholesome casseroles.

SOLDIER: It's in her own interests.

FATHER: I'm now not so concerned for the state of the world.

SOLDIER: Soon she will see.

FATHER: Since what can you do, tell me…

SOLDIER: The time has now come!

FATHER: What can you do?

SOLDIER: To be happy at last.

FATHER: We must all now be happy.

SOLDIER: To be happy and free.

FATHER: Be happy and free.

> *The MOTHER stands, in deep shock. She wrestles with her agony.*
>
> *The GIRL screams from the darkness.*
>
> *The sound of a newborn screaming.*
>
> *After a time the screaming suddenly stops.*

A deep silence falls.

The MOTHER disappears into the darkness.

The sound of an army marching past.

The MOTHER appears with a swaddled baby. She hands the baby to the SOLDIER.

SOLDIER: His eyes are so like hers. But why though does he stare like this? Why are his eyes so unblinking, so fixed? My beautiful child, my beautiful child, my future, my future, my future, my…

The FATHER uncorks the champagne. Instead of the pop we hear the loud crack of a gunshot.

The GIRL is revealed on the bed, a gaping bullet-hole in her forehead, blood everywhere, the flowers strewn over the body.

The sound of the army marching increases in volume and then blackout.